Project RED (Revolutionizing EDucation)

"Project RED's findings reinforce the significance of strong leadership at all levels. This is an important and valuable report."

> —Bill Hamilton, Superintendent
> Walled Lake Consolidated Schools, Walled Lake, Michigan

"We've needed a metastudy of 1-to-1 programs and ubiquitous technologies for years, but none existed till now. Project RED's research is rich, deep, practical, and meaningful, with the kind of specifics educators require to carry forward 1-to-1 programs for fundamental improvement."

> —Pamela Livingston
> Author, *1-to-1 Learning: Laptop Programs That Work*

"At a time when it is needed the most, Project RED brings together student achievement and cost-effectiveness. The concept of radical educational reform has been discussed for years. Now, Project RED provides the blueprint for reform success, providing a much greater return on our investments in education."

> —John Musso, Executive Director
> Association for School Business Officials International

"Project RED is nothing less than a blueprint for remaking American education."

> —Angus King
> Former Governor of Maine

"Our students are different, and they need different learning opportunities. This report [Project RED] provides insight into how educational technology can power those new learning opportunities."

> —Anita Givens, Associate Commissioner
> Standards and Programs, Texas Education Agency

Revolutionizing Education through Technology

"If technology is to be truly effective, it must be carefully and thoughtfully woven into the entire fabric of the school and learning. Done right, it changes both the appearance and nature of education."

> —Calvin Baker, Superintendent
> Vail School District, Vail, Arizona

"Technology can play a huge role in increasing educational productivity, but not just as an add-on or for a high-tech reproduction of current practice. Again, we need to change the underlying processes to leverage the capabilities of technology. The military calls it a force multiplier. Better use of online learning, virtual schools, and other smart uses of technology is not so much about replacing educational roles as it is about giving each person the tools they need to be more successful—reducing wasted time, energy, and money.

"By far, the best strategy for boosting productivity is to leverage transformational change in the educational system to improve outcomes for children. To do so requires a fundamental rethinking of the structure and delivery of education in the United States."

—The New Normal: Doing More with Less
Remarks of U.S. Secretary of Education Arne Duncan
American Enterprise Institute Panel, "Bang for the Buck in Schooling," November 17, 2010

"Teachers find more ways to connect with their students with modern technology. With many more creative ways to teach and learn, teachers want to share and spend more time investing in themselves and their classroom."

—Kip Keckler, Instructional Technology Teacher
Washington Middle School, Kenosha, Wisconsin

"One-to-one computing transforms the classroom from teacher-centered to student-centered by placing the technology in the hands of the students. No longer is the teacher the purveyor of knowledge but a facilitator, learning along with the students."

—Alice Owen, Executive Director of Technology
Irving Intermediate School District, Irving, Texas

"We are experiencing cost savings by having students create electronic student handbooks and store them on their mobile learning devices, and by sending homework electronically and eliminating the use of notebook paper or printer paper."

—Kyle Menchhofer, District Technology Coordinator
St. Marys City Schools, St. Marys, Ohio

"Students who are behind their peers are more likely to drop out. Through the use of technology we are able to help them graduate with their friends, and their self-esteem increases as they see their progress."

—Rosemary Williams, Principal
Burkeville High School, Burkeville, Texas

"As we manage the transition from predominantly print-based classrooms to digital learning environments, we have the opportunity to truly personalize learning, engaging and inspiring students everywhere."

—Karen Cator, Director of the Office of Educational Technology
U.S. Department of Education

Revolutionizing
Education
through
Technology

The Project RED
Roadmap for
Transformation

Thomas W. Greaves
Jeanne Hayes
Leslie Wilson
Michael Gielniak
Eric L. Peterson

International Society for Technology in Education
EUGENE, OREGON • WASHINGTON, DC

Revolutionizing Education through Technology
The Project RED Roadmap for Transformation

Thomas W. Greaves, Jeanne Hayes, Leslie Wilson, Michael Gielniak, and Eric L. Peterson

Content © The Greaves Group, The Hayes Connection, and One-to-One Institute

Paperback edition © 2012 International Society for Technology in Education

Director of Book Publishing: *Courtney Burkholder*
Acquisitions Editor: *Jeff V. Bolkan*
Production Editors: *Lynda Gansel, Tina Wells*
Production Coordinator: *Emily Reed*
Graphic Designer: *Signe Landin*
Developmental Editor: *Mike van Mantgem*
Copy Editor and Book Production: *Tracy Cozzens*
Cover and Book Design: *Signe Landin*

First Edition
ISBN: 978-1-56484-322-7
Printed in the United States of America

ISTE® is a registered trademark of the International Society for Technology in Education.

This book is based on *The Technology Factor: Nine Keys to Student Achievement and Cost-Effectiveness*, MDR, 2010, © The Greaves Group, The Hayes Connection, and One-to-One Institute.

About ISTE

The International Society for Technology in Education (ISTE) is the trusted source for professional development, knowledge generation, advocacy, and leadership for innovation. ISTE is the premier membership association for educators and education leaders engaged in improving teaching and learning by advancing the effective use of technology in PK–12 and teacher education.

Home to ISTE's annual conference and exposition, the ISTE leadership conference, and the widely adopted NETS, ISTE represents more than 100,000 professionals worldwide. We support our members with information, networking opportunities, and guidance as they face the challenge of transforming education. To find out more about these and other ISTE initiatives, visit our website at www.iste.org.

As part of our mission, ISTE Book Publishing works with experienced educators to develop and produce practical resources for classroom teachers, teacher educators, and technology leaders. Every manuscript we select for publication is carefully peer-reviewed and professionally edited. We value your feedback on this book and other ISTE products. E-mail us at books@iste.org.

International Society for Technology in Education
Washington, DC, Office:
    1710 Rhode Island Ave. NW, Suite 900, Washington, DC 20036-3132
Eugene, Oregon, Office:
    180 West 8th Ave., Suite 300, Eugene, OR 97401-2916
Order Desk: 1.800.336.5191
Order Fax: 1.541.302.3778
Customer Service: orders@iste.org
Book Publishing: books@iste.org
Book Sales and Marketing: booksmarketing@iste.org
Web: www.iste.org

About the Project RED Team

Thomas W. Greaves
Chief Executive Officer and Founder, The Greaves Group

Tom is recognized as a visionary in the conceptualization, design, engineering, and marketing of technologies for schools. He holds multiple patents and patent disclosures for student-computing technologies and has been involved in hundreds of 1-to-1 computing projects at the district, state, and federal levels. He has published widely and is currently the Software Information Industry Association (SIIA) Mobile Computing Trends Watch Report editor. Along with Jeanne Hayes, he is coauthor of the 2006 and 2008 *America's Digital Schools* surveys.

Tom has 44 years of experience in the computer industry, including 26 years at IBM, where he was a member of the IBM EduQuest senior management team. In 1996, he cofounded NetSchools, the first company to focus on comprehensive curriculum-integrated, Internet-connected 1-to-1 laptop solutions. He now leads The Greaves Group, a strategic education consulting organization. Tom is the recipient of the prestigious 2010 SIIA Ed Tech Impact Award and is a well-known speaker and panelist.

Jeanne Hayes
President, The Hayes Connection

Jeanne established The Hayes Connection in 2005 to serve education market companies and school districts, based on her 30 years of experience in creating school databases, analyzing market trends, and helping clients market to schools at Quality Education Data (QED), which she founded in 1981.

A former educator and debate coach, Jeanne has testified before Congress and speaks at conferences nationwide about instructional technology and other education issues. She is coauthor with Tom Greaves of the 2006 and 2008 *America's Digital Schools* surveys. She has served as a board member of the CEO Forum on Education and Technology, the Consortium for School Networking (CoSN), and the Education Section of SIIA. She was recognized as the CoSN Private Sector Champion for 2002, one of the *Converge* magazine's "Those Who Make a Difference 2000," and one of the *eSchool News'* Impact 30 for 2001. In 2002, Jeanne was inducted into the Association of Educational Publishers' Hall of Fame.

Leslie Wilson
Chief Executive Officer, One-to-One Institute

Leslie is a founding member of the One-to-One Institute, where she created the highly effective programs and services model based on the Michigan Freedom to Learn Program. She now leads the institute's leadership team and works with a collaborative cadre of state and national service providers. Leslie is a thought leader in the 1-to-1 community and a tireless advocate for ubiquitous technology at the state, national, and international levels. She provides assistance with the planning, design and launch, curriculum and content integration, online assessment, leadership, and sustainability of 1-to-1 programs.

Leslie served in public education for 31 years in seven school districts. As cochair of the National Steering Committee of One-to-One Directors, she facilitates networking and collaboration among 1-to-1 visionaries. She is a well-known presenter on educational transformation topics and serves on numerous national and state committees and advisory boards.

Michael Gielniak, PhD
Director of Programs and Development, One-to-One Institute

Michael is a key member of the One-to-One Institute leadership team, responsible for the creation, implementation, and oversight of the institute's professional learning activities, new programs, fund development, and research activities. Before joining the institute, he served as the executive director at the Anton Art Center and the Center for Creative Learning and Teaching.

Both a Fulbright Scholar and an Emmy Award winner, Michael has worked with creative and educational environments around the globe for 25 years. As a consultant to the Macomb Intermediate School District, he developed the Macomb New Teacher Academy, where he trained more than 1,000 teachers. He has worked with the Michigan Department of Education on a variety of projects since 2003. He managed the development of arts content for the Clarifying Language in Michigan Benchmarks (MIClimb); served on the rubric development committee for the Michigan school assessment program, Education, Yes!; and was a reviewer for Michigan's teacher preparation standards.

Eric L. Peterson
President and Chief Executive Officer, Peterson Public Sector Consulting
Advisor to One-to-One Institute

Eric has worked with the Michigan Departments of Education, Treasury, and Management and Budget, as well as with Michigan legislators and Michigan House and Senate fiscal agencies, for more than 19 years. In his work with more than 500 school districts, he has developed numerous techniques for customizing operational, instructional, and financial solutions. Most recently, he assisted the Detroit Public Schools, in partnership with another consulting firm, in the district's quest to right-size the organization and reduce debt.

A frequent presenter at national and state-level conferences, Eric performs process and organizational studies for public schools and businesses throughout Michigan. In 2004, he received the Distinguished Service Award from the Michigan School Business Officials board of directors for 13 years of outstanding support to Michigan school business officials.

Acknowledgments

Project RED (Revolutionizing EDucation) was inspired by the desire to contribute to the reengineering of education through research and through sharing compelling stories of transformation.

First, and most importantly, we express our appreciation to the more than 1,000 principals and other school administrators who took the time to complete a challenging survey. Without their work, we would have no findings.

Our sponsors were a tremendous help, and we are most grateful for their faith and foresight in funding an important piece of research. Our thanks go to Eileen Lento's team at Intel, Karen Cator's (before she advanced to the U.S. Department of Education) and David Byer's team at Apple, Mark Nieker's team at the Pearson Foundation, Sharon Montgomery's team at Qwest Communications, and Martin Brutosky's team at eChalk. In particular, our lead sponsor, Intel, pushed us and supported us in every way. Chris Brown of Pearson Education and Paul Kuhne of eChalk contributed materially to the quality of the final product. And Kathy Hurley of the Pearson Foundation made many contributions to the success of the project.

Our supporting organizations also provided strong support throughout the process. In particular, Ann Flynn of the NSBA, Doug Levin of SETDA, Irene Spero and Keith Krueger of CoSN, and Mark Schneiderman of SIIA provided valuable resources and thoughtful insights.

Diane Rapley, chief editor of our original report, and Dan Hoffman of the University of Denver, our crosstabs expert, provided invaluable assistance and wisdom that went well beyond their job descriptions. John Greaves gave us eye-opening insights into the power of predictive modeling and principle component analysis. Ian Hickey, our chief technical officer, could always be counted on to handle all things technical, from the website to the database. And Rodney Muth, professor of administrative leadership and policy studies at the University of Colorado, Denver's School of Education and Human Development, provided advice as an education and statistics expert as well as a careful and subtle review of our draft report.

Fady Khairallah and our friends from MDR—a company that maintains the most robust database of schools in the nation—exceeded our expectations at every turn. They put tremendous data resources at our disposal, and they took on the key role of designing and publishing the original report. Moira McArdle and Colleen Galligan provided marketing insight and design savvy to the data-heavy original report.

Thanks also to the International Society for Technology in Education and Intel for publishing this paperback edition of our report.

And, finally, to our spouses, whose counsel and patience can only be described as exemplary: Vylee Greaves; Tom Olkowski, PhD; and Samantha Gielniak.

To each of you, and to the many others who contributed to the quality of the work, we say thank you!

Thomas W. Greaves
Jeanne Hayes
Leslie Wilson
Michael Gielniak
Eric L. Peterson

Project RED Sponsors and Supporting Organizations

Sponsors

Intel (2011–13)

Apple (2011–12)

eChalk (2011–12)

HP (2012–13)

Pearson (2011–13)

Qwest Communications (2011–12)

SMART Technologies (2012–13)

Supporting Organizations

American Association of School Administrators (AASA)

Association of Educational Publishers (AEP)

Association of Educational Service Agencies (AESA)

Association of School Business Officials (ASBO)

Consortium for School Networking (CoSN)

The International Association for K–12 Online Learning (iNACOL)

International Society for Technology in Education (ISTE)

The National Association of Media & Technology Centers (NAMTC)

National School Boards Association (NSBA)

Software & Information Industry Association (SIIA)

State Educational Technology Directors Association (SETDA)

Publication of this book was made possible in part by the generous support of Intel.

Contents

Contents

Foreword

"Project RED is nothing less than a blueprint for remaking American education—second-order change—not through more or better testing, charter schools, longer school days, more or even better teachers, but through fundamentally altering how we do education, the first real change in the process of education itself in a thousand years."

—Angus King
Governor of Maine, 1995–2003

Economic competition is global, focused, and unrelenting; there is no such thing as a "safe" job. Whatever it was that formed the basis of your state's economy 50, 25, or even 10 years ago is now at risk; and whatever it is that is coming next is hard to see or define, let alone prepare for.

This came home to me in the late 1990s when the bloom of the dotcom bubble was beginning to fade, and the call-center jobs we all thought were the next phase of industrialism were disappearing almost as fast as they had come. It suddenly hit me that I had no idea what the citizens of my state were going to do for a living 20 (or even 10) years from now. And the events of the past 10 years have only intensified this sense—and my conclusion that the recession we have been in for the past few years is more structural than cyclical.

The fact is that everybody in the world wants our jobs and the standard of living that comes with them, and for the first time ever, they have the means to take them.

So, what do we do? Denial is always an option (probably the most common one at this moment), but that is surely not going to help us adapt to the new reality all around us. As my father used to say, no decision is a decision, and it is usually the wrong one.

Another option is to meet what is fundamentally an economic challenge with economic remedies—tax cuts and incentives; a new round of protectionism; lower interest rates; "streamlining" regulation; scouring public budgets for "fraud, waste, and abuse"; credit enhancements; investment in research and development—in other words, the usual suspects. These may be helpful on the margins, but none individually—or even the whole list—will fundamentally alter the trajectory of 21st-century history, which is inevitably in the direction of intensifying global competition.

As I learned when I read the Project RED report, steps like these, while important and maybe even occasionally useful, represent "first-order change"—incremental improvement but not the kind of transformative action necessary to meet major, disruptive challenges. Sandbags and shelters are sufficient for most storms, but as we learned, when a Katrina hits, we need a whole new level of response.

And make no mistake, we are in the midst of an economic Katrina—huge, inexorable, and deadly—and it threatens to sweep away with it a great deal of what we have come to believe is our birthright.

But I believe there is something, actually one thing, we can and must do to give ourselves a fighting chance—dramatically improve both the output and efficiency of our schools. We cannot compete on wages or access to natural resources or capital, and besides, those are the currency of the age just past. The new competition is in innovation and invention, creativity, productivity, and vision. And the wellspring of all of these is learning—history and language, science and math, drama, music, and dance. We are seeing the fruition of the promise—and the threat—of industrialism. A person's economic future depends on brains, not brawn, and the best brains, or maybe more accurately, the best trained brains, will win.

But it is not about cramming more physics or Spanish into 16-year-old heads; it is about giving them the tools and techniques to teach themselves, both in school and beyond. In this connection, my friend Seymour Papert made the most profound observation I have run across on 21st-century education: "It is no longer good enough for schools to send out students who know how to do what they were taught. The modern world needs citizens who can do what they were not taught. We call this *learning learning.*

To achieve this, we need change that is big and transformational, not gradual and incremental. It means twice the educational output, however measured, at something less than today's cost. It also means educational equity on an unprecedented scale; given the stakes, we simply cannot afford the massive waste of talent represented by failing schools and lost communities. And it means education that is at once more rigorous and more engaging, more collaborative and more inclusive.

Which brings me to this report.

Project RED is nothing less than a blueprint for remaking American education—second-order change—not through more or better testing, charter schools, longer school days, more or even better teachers, but through fundamentally altering how we do education, the first real change in the process of education itself in a thousand years.

The authors did not create this blueprint out of whole cloth and present it to us here as the latest in what seems to be a semi-annual iteration of "school reform"; instead, it is the product of old-fashioned research—a hard analytical look at what is working in schools and school districts around the country. And what is working is ubiquitous technology (a fancy way of saying that every kid has a laptop) fully integrated into the classroom by well-prepared and well-led teachers. The closer the student–computer ratio gets to 1-to-1, the better the results; the better prepared the teachers are to take full advantage of the potential of the technology, the better the results; and the stronger the leadership of the process by the principal, the better the results.

In a sense, I have been waiting for this report for 10 years. It, along with the pioneering work of people like David Silvernail here in Maine, confirms what a small group (and I am not kidding when I say small) thought back in 2000—that a digital device in the hands of every student made total sense and was the tool upon which a truly transformed educational system could be built.

But the report also underlines our major learning here in Maine—that the computer is the necessary starting place, but alone is not sufficient to generate the transformational change we so desperately need. What we have learned is that it is all about the teachers and the leadership in the school; with great professional development and a new pedagogy, amazing things happen, but just handing out the laptops is not going to do it.

In this sense, Project RED confirms one of my most deeply held convictions about successful leadership—that execution is as important as vision. The vision of a digital device in the hands of every student, providing access to all the world, is a powerful idea, but it fails utterly if the network is down or the screen freezes or the teacher is unschooled in the techniques of technology integration. Through painstaking work, the authors here tease out the factors that can and do make it work—from school leadership to professional development to simple reliability and on down the list.

Angus King
Governor of Maine, 1995–2003

INTRODUCTION

Project RED:
An Education Revolution

We are Project RED! What is Project RED? We conducted a national survey to analyze what's working in technology-transformed schools and to show how technology can save money when properly implemented.

- We researched more than a thousand schools that provide access to the Internet for every student. We asked them what factors contributed to the success or failure of their programs.

- We're looking for other technology-transformed schools that we may have overlooked so we can have the most complete database ever assembled from which to learn.

- We're also searching for proof of cost savings from the implementation of technology in any K–12 environment, whether these savings come from online learning courses, professional development, concurrent enrollment in college courses, data mapping, special needs programs, or any other program.

We learned (and are continuing to learn) many important things from our work on Project RED, and we'll discuss them in chapters to come, but there are three key insights we want you to embrace. These insights are invaluable to leaders planning to implement ubiquitous technology in schools, and we'll return to them again and again:

- Properly implemented educational technology can substantially improve student achievement.

- Properly implemented educational technology can be revenue positive at all levels—national, state, and local.

- Continuous access to a computing device for every student leads to increased academic achievement and financial benefits, especially when technology is properly implemented.

We hope this book will convince you of the truth of these insights. An education revolution will happen only with the support of leadership. You, as an educational leader, must break the trail. Real change requires that every segment of the educational community commit to the change and then follow through.

Goals of Project RED

Although data gathered over the years have indicated that technology has not achieved the same impact in education as in other sectors of the economy, it has become clear that a few pockets of excellence are successfully transforming schools with technology using specific implementation strategies. The urgent need to understand those successful implementation strategies provided the impetus for Project RED.

America's Digital Schools 2008 (Greaves & Hayes, 2008) had revealed that only 33% of school districts with 1-to-1 schools considered their academic improvement due to technology to be significant: the Project RED team saw this as an opportunity to identify the strategies behind those improvements and provide guidelines for other schools. This became the first goal of the survey.

In *The Price We Pay: Economic and Social Consequences of Inadequate Education*, the authors pointed out the connections between education and the economy (Belfield & Levin, 2007), so Project RED established a second goal: to research the potentially positive financial impact of technology in schools. Surprisingly, unlike in the private sector, very little research has been done on the financial impact of technology in education.

Because debate in recent years has questioned whether students perform better when they have continuous access to a computing device, Project RED established a third goal: to examine the impact of 1-to-1 computing on student performance and education budgets.

Many studies, including earlier research by the authors, have addressed district-level activities and the importance of district-level leadership. However, Project RED deliberately adopted a school-level focus in order to observe principal, student, and teacher behaviors as closely as possible; correlate student performance to school-level activities; and ensure that school-to-school implementation variances did not mask correlations to student performance.

Scope

Many surveys and studies have examined the impact of educational technology. Unfortunately, most have covered only one school or a few schools, and the study interest areas have covered only a sparse matrix. Project RED provides unprecedented scope, breadth, and depth:

- 997 schools, representative of the U.S. school universe, and 49 states and the District of Columbia
- 11 diverse education success measures
- 22 categories of independent variables, with many subcategories
- Comparison of findings by student–computer ratios (1-to-1, 2-to-1, 3-to-1, etc.)
- Comprehensive demographic data correlated to survey results

Given the array of factors and variables, a variety of analysis techniques were required, including regression analysis, principal component analysis, and predictive modeling (see www.projectred.org for more information on our methodology). The survey has been augmented by interviews and additional information, generously provided by school and district administrators.

Project RED's findings and recommendations will assist four groups—legislatures, federal and state agencies, school districts, and industry—in remaking the American education system and re-engineering our schools. Our findings will give you the information you need to be confident as you make critical decisions.

Legislatures. Education is one of the largest budget items for every state. Project RED will introduce legislatures to the cost savings and return on investment (ROI) that result from effective technology implementation as part of education reform. Project RED's findings can also help support legislative action that removes barriers to new educational practices.

Federal and state agencies. Groups such as the National Governors Association, the Council of Chief State School Officers, and other education leadership associations (many of whom supported Project RED's research), are interested in understanding the cost savings and increased student achievement associated with effective technology initiatives. Project RED will help these groups identify an action agenda they can share with their memberships.

School districts. Superintendents are under pressure from a variety of sources to improve outcomes while doing more with less funding. Properly implemented technology initiatives have a positive impact on Education Success Measures (ESM) and save money over the long run. The models and strategies provided by Project RED can be helpful to these leaders when implementing technology.

Industry. Publishers and producers of hardware, software, and infrastructure products and services must understand trends and differences among various segments in the education market. This understanding allows business leaders to best address American education needs for the 21st century.

The goal of this book is to empower education leaders, policy makers, and industry to effect meaningful change in American schools. To effect this change, each stakeholder group must have a shared vision that transcends mandate, function, or official capacity. Project RED's findings provide the foundation for this shared vision.

For more about Project RED—who we are and what we do—see Appendix A or visit the Project RED website (www.projectred.org).

CHAPTER **1**

First- and Second-Order Change

In early 2009, all indicators pointed to a perfect storm on the horizon in the U.S. education system. Although the requirements for student achievement had been increasing, student performance remained essentially flat, despite the fact that education spending had increased at more than twice the rate of inflation between 1965 and 2005. In addition, the advent of the Internet had widened the gap between the requirements for student achievement and actual student performance to an unacceptable degree. The implosion of the economy created an additional storm front, and it appeared that the financial picture for schools was unlikely to improve for decades, if at all. The U.S. Department of Education was explicit about future education funding. "Plan on doing more with less" was the order of the day. A radical response is needed to address this situation.

However, in today's educational landscape, very little effort is directed toward radical improvements, where students learn at twice the rate and half the cost, for example, as outlined in the fourth grand challenge of the 2010 National Educational Technology Plan.

*The Project RED team estimates that first-order educational change yields savings of $30 billion a year at best—while second-order change could yield savings of **$100 billion a year or more** and significantly improve student performance.*

Project RED provides a radical response to the situation faced by U.S. schools today—a way for school districts and policy leaders to begin to address the grand challenge and navigate the perfect storm successfully using second-order change principles. Intrigued? Read on for a discussion of first-order and second-order change.

First-Order Change

Within the change cycle in any industry or endeavor, incremental first-order changes and intervening plateaus are generally followed by transformative second-order changes. What is the difference? A simple way to determine first-order change is by examining potential outcomes. If the proposed change does not have the potential to cause a twofold (or more) improvement, then that change can be safely classified as a first-order change. Almost all educational technology initiatives have been first-order changes. Even if these changes are well implemented, impact will always be limited.

> *First-order* changes are reforms that assume that the existing organizational goals and structures are basically adequate and what needs to be done is to correct deficiencies in policies and practice. Engineers would label such changes as solutions to quality control problems.
>
> For schools, such planned changes would include recruiting better teachers and administrators; raising salaries; distributing resources equitably; selecting better texts, materials, and supplies; and adding new or deleting old content and courses to and from the curriculum.
>
> When such improvements occur, the results frequently appear to be fundamental changes or even appear to be changes in core activities, but actually these changes do little to alter basic school structures of how time and space are used or how students and teachers are organized and assigned.
>
> First-order changes, then, try to make what exists more efficient and effective without disrupting basic organizational arrangements or how people perform their roles.
>
> —Larry Cuban
> *The Managerial Imperative and the Practice of Leadership in Schools,* 1988, pp. 228–229

Second-Order Change

Second-order change implies a fundamental or significant break with past and current practices. This type of change represents a dramatic difference in current practices. Second-order changes require new knowledge and skills for successful implementation. Project RED defines second-order change for our schools as follows:

- Student performance levels double, at a minimum.

- The change mechanism is broad scale and addresses all student populations.

- The changes are scalable to the largest educational entities.

- Changes are sustainable and can withstand the vagaries of the economy, teacher and staff turnover, and other factors.

Examples of second-order change in schools are as follows:

- Mechanisms in place to address each student with personalized instruction programs.

- Exchange of seat-time requirements for demonstrated proficiency in coursework.

- Change in focus to student as customer.

Second-order change is extremely difficult to achieve, but the results are game-changing. Project RED data illustrate that substantial improvements in academic-success measures and financial return on investment (ROI) are tied to second-order changes, wherein the re-engineering of schools is facilitated by the judicious use of ubiquitous technology. Interestingly, Project RED data indicate that it may actually be impossible to achieve second-order change in schools with a student–computer ratio higher than one student per computer (1-to-1).

> *Second-order* changes, on the other hand, aim at altering the fundamental ways of achieving organizational goals because of major dissatisfaction with current arrangements. Second-order changes introduce new goals and interventions that transform the familiar way of doing things into novel solutions to persistent problems.... Engineers would call these solutions to design problems.... The history of school reform has been largely first-order improvements on the basic structures of schooling established in the late 19th century.
>
> —Larry Cuban
> *The Managerial Imperative and the Practice of Leadership in Schools,* 1988, pp. 229–230

The table below shows some more ways to differentiate between first-order change and second order change.

Differentiating between First- and Second-Order Change

First-Order Change	Second-Order Change
An extension of the past	A break with the past
Consistent with prevailing organizational norms	Inconsistent with prevailing organizational norms
Congruent with personal values	Incongruent with personal values
Easily learned using existing knowledge	Requires new knowledge and skills

School Leadership That Works, *McREL, 2005. Source: Project RED (www.projectred.org)*

Magnitude of Change

Magnitude of change refers not to the size of the change but rather the implications of the change for those who are expected to implement it or will be affected by it. It is important to note that the magnitude of change lies in the eye of the beholder and that the same change may have different implications for different stakeholders. Our research suggests that leaders need to understand whether changes are first or second order for staff members and differentiate their leadership styles accordingly.

Conclusion

We believe second-order change is possible: Student performance levels will double, and at the same time costs will go down. Project RED's findings and recommendations can serve as your guide! Read on for a discussion of our major findings.

CHAPTER 2

The Major Findings of Project RED

We launched Project RED because we were curious. We knew that some schools were having amazing results with their technology implementation programs, while others were experiencing nothing but frustration and disappointment. The following inquiries informed the direction of our research:

- We set out to identify the technology implementation strategies that can successfully transform American schools.

- We isolated the variables that were having the greatest impact in order to create impactful guidelines for schools.

- We researched the potentially positive financial impact of successful technology implementations in schools.

- We specifically looked at the impact of 1-to-1 computing on student performance and education budgets.

Many studies, including earlier research by Project RED team members, have addressed district-level activities and the importance of district-level leadership. However, with Project RED we deliberately adopted a school-level focus in order to observe principal, student, and teacher behaviors as closely as possible; correlate student performance to school-level activities; and ensure that school-to-school implementation variances did not mask correlations to student performance.

An analysis of the Project RED data revealed seven major findings of interest to schools embarking on or already administering a technology implementation.

- Proper implementation of technology is linked to education success.

- Properly implemented technology saves money.

- 1-to-1 schools that properly implement technology outperform all other schools, including all other 1-to-1 schools.

- A school principal's ability to lead is critical to the success of an implementation effort.

- Technology-transformed intervention improves learning.

- Online collaboration increases learning productivity and student engagement.

- Daily use of technology delivers the best return on investment (ROI).

Let's take a closer look at each of these findings.

Proper implementation of technology is linked to education success.

Educational technology best practices have a significant positive impact on improvements in student achievement, and must be widely and consistently practiced.

Effective technology implementation in schools is a complex puzzle. Hundreds of interrelated factors play a role. The presence of computers in a school does not guarantee improved student achievement. Indeed, providing every student a computer is the beginning, not the end, of improving student performance. In fact, schools with a 1-to-1 student–computer ratio that address only a few of these key factors perform only marginally better than non–1-to-1 schools.

Ultimately, the implementation of best practices is as important as the technology itself; and the value of technology in terms of student achievement depends on the quality of its implementation. In Chapter 3 you'll find a list of some of our most important recommendations that correlate with success, the Project RED Key Implementation Factors.

Properly implemented technology saves money.

The richer the technology implementation, the more positive the direct cost reductions and indirect revenue enhancements.

The education sector has often failed to experience transformation through the use of technology. This failure is due, in large part, to the challenge—real or perceived—of allocating the necessary initial capital budget to start such initiatives.

An understanding of the financial benefits of technology is surprisingly absent in schools. The prevailing wisdom is that educational technology is an expensive proposition. However, Project RED data support the business case that there is enough money in the system at a macro level to properly implement technology and positively impact many Education Success Measures (ESMs), from high-stakes tests to disciplinary actions.

The incremental cost of a ubiquitous technology implementation, including hardware, software, professional development, and training and support, is roughly $100 to $400 per student per year, depending on the school's starting point. The positive impact could be as high as $56,437 per student per year, depending on the school and state, after accounting for the full impact of a career lifetime of increased tax revenues. This number is based in large part on schools as we know them. In second-order change schools, it is likely that the impact would be higher.

Under today's system, if money is saved via technology, the dollars saved will not go to the school's bank account. Given the significant shortfalls in school funding today, schools spend all the money they get. But the savings earned through properly implemented technology initiatives will allow schools to move the dollars closer to students and moderate the effects of economic downturns. The challenge is to encourage schools to adopt cost-saving measures along with mechanisms for capturing the savings, so that the savings do not disappear into the system.

Properly implemented educational technology can be revenue positive at all levels—national, state, and local. For best results, stakeholders need to invest in the re-engineering of schools, not just in technology itself.

The financial impacts of properly implemented technology include direct cost reductions as well as indirect revenue enhancements that are only realizable at the state level. Examples of state-level costs that can be saved include moving from paper-based to electronic high-stakes tests, and the reteaching of students who fail courses.

Project RED estimates that 1-to-1 high schools with a properly implemented learning management system (LMS) could cut their copy budgets in half. Labor accounts for roughly 50% of the total cost for copying. Assuming the cost of operating and maintaining a copy machine is $100,000 per year for a 1,500-student high school, on a national basis this equates to a savings of $739 million per year for high schools alone.

The economic cost of student dropouts is well known. An individual's lifetime tax revenues track with his or her level of education. Nationally, if 25% of dropouts graduated from high school, and 25% of those individuals then graduated from college, the increase in tax revenue would be $77 billion per year per graduating class. In this scenario, the aggregate positive financial impact of all students after 40 years would be $3 trillion per year.

1-to-1 Schools that employ the Project RED Key Implementation Factors outperform all schools, including all other 1-to-1 schools.

> *A 1-to-1 student–computer ratio has a higher impact on student outcomes and financial benefits than higher ratios.*

A bleak long-term economic outlook may have an impact on the adoption of educational technology, which is considered by many to be an expensive proposition for schools. Certainly, 1-to-1 computing is more expensive than a 3-to-1 deployment in terms of initial outlay. This cost barrier for a 1-to-1 deployment, while very real, is only one consideration. Device costs and total costs of ownership are declining, and it can be argued that connectivity, application availability, community of practice, and the knowledge base in schools for successful implementation provide benefits far beyond the costs associated with an initial outlay for a 1-to-1 deployment.

Interestingly, the data show that 2-to-1 schools resemble 3-to-1 or higher-ratio schools more closely than 1-to-1 schools. Schools with a 1-to-1 student–computer ratio may be fundamentally different in a pedagogical sense. Indeed, a 1-to-1 student–computer ratio has a greater impact on student outcomes and financial benefits than other ratios, and the Key Implementation Factors detailed in the first finding increase both benefits. In general, schools with a 1-to-1 student–computer ratio outperform non–1-to-1 schools on both academic and financial measures. Moreover, a number of positive financial implications that are attached to 1-to-1 computing, particularly when properly implemented, reveal that 1-to-1 adoption rates should increase, especially as costs come down and more schools become comfortable with technology.

Project RED has selected four of 11 Education Success Measures to illustrate the impact of 1-to-1 deployments. The accompanying table shows the percentage of Project RED respondents reporting improvements in ESMs from technology deployments.

1-to-1 Works When Properly Implemented

Education Success Measure (ESM)	Properly Implemented 1-to-1 Schools (%)	All 1-to-1 Schools (%)	All Other Schools (%)
Reduction: Disciplinary action	92	65	50
Increase: High-stakes test scores	90	70	69
Reduction: Dropout rate	89	58	45
Increase: Graduation rate	63	57	51

Source: Project RED (www.projectred.org)

Schools with a 1-to-1 student–computer ratio that practice the top four implementation factors identified by Project RED experience the most positive improvements. The top four implementation factors are intervention classes that use technology every class; principal leads change management training at least monthly; online collaboration among students daily; core curriculum using technology at least weekly. (See Chapter 3 for a discussion of all nine of the Key Implementation Factors.)

- 92% report disciplinary action reduction
- 90% report high-stakes test scores increase
- 89% report dropout rate reduction
- 63% report graduation rate increase

All 1-to-1 Schools

Schools with a 1-to-1 student–computer ratio without proper implementation of technology experience positive results, but those results significantly lag behind those 1-to-1 schools with proper implementation.

- 65% report disciplinary action reduction
- 70% report high-stakes test scores increase
- 58% report dropout rate reduction
- 57% report graduation rate increase

Non–1-to-1 Schools

Schools without a 1-to-1 student–computer ratio benefit from the use of technology, but the benefits lag behind 1-to-1 schools.

- 50% report disciplinary action reduction

- 69% report high-stakes test scores increase

- 45% report dropout rate reduction

- 51% report graduation rate increase

These data make it clear that 1-to-1 is the way to go, and 1-to-1 is leveraged fully only when Project RED's Key Implementation Factors are present.

The principal's ability to lead is critical to the success of an implementation effort.

Change must be modeled and championed at the top.

Strong, district leadership is essential for successful schools. All levels of district leadership are important, individually and collectively, including school boards, superintendents, and assistant superintendents for curriculum, instruction, technology, finance, and operations. However, the principal is the primary influence of professional development within a school. The quality of a principal's leadership has a major impact on education technology usage, leading to improved student outcomes. Many educators agree that it is impossible for their school to rise above the capabilities of the principal. Key measures of principal effectiveness in terms of technology use include the following:

- Skillful change leadership

- Conceptual and tactical understanding

- Real system reform versus tinkering around the edges

- Communication about best practices

- A shared and inspiring vision

- Stakeholder buy-in

- Consistent, open communication with and among stakeholders

- Planning for technology acquisition, implementation, and assessment

How well principals guide the professional learning process of education technology use has consequences in terms of time, cost, and results. A principal must effectively perform the following:

- Model technology use

- Enable teacher collaboration time

- Enable online professional learning

- Use change management strategies

- Enable regularly scheduled professional learning opportunities for teachers

Project RED data show that, within schools, the principal is one of the most important variables across the 11 Education Success Measures. Principals have a major impact on technology use in schools, and hence student outcomes. This finding suggests that change leadership training for principals is of paramount importance.

The accompanying table shows the percentage of Project RED respondents who reported benefits of a technology implementation, in this case in terms of disciplinary action reductions.

Example of Improvement Attributed to Technology and Principal Leadership

Measure	All Schools (%)	All 1-to-1 Schools (%)	1-to-1 Schools with Principal Change Management Training (%)
Reduction: Disciplinary action	50	65	73

Source: Project RED (www.projectred.org)

Principals must lead the change management that is required to transform a school. Principals must also lead in the use of data to inform instruction, and must champion the movement from teacher-led to student-centered instruction. These skills may be new to principals who, in traditional industrial-age schools, have long served primarily as managers.

In decentralized school systems, principals are also important in terms of financial improvement. As the trend to decentralization continues, teachers may continue to use, for example, traditional paper-intensive copier-based solutions unless the principal models desired technology-use behaviors. Technology-forward principals lead by sending out meeting notices via email instead of hard copy, host online collaborative discussions and communities of practice, and perform classroom observations to ensure technology is being properly used.

Thus, while all schools benefit from a technology implementation, when principals receive specialized training, and technology is properly implemented, the benefits increase even more.

Technology-transformed intervention improves learning.

Technology-transformed intervention classes are an important component in improving student outcomes.

Project RED defines technology-transformed intervention classes as those in which technology plays an integral role in learning. Generally, it is a learning environment in which every student has a computer and the curriculum is delivered electronically. The teacher spends most of his or her class time in one-on-one interactions with students, or conducts class in small-group mode. Each student progresses at his or her own pace.

Project RED found that technology-transformed intervention classes, including English language learners, Title I, special education, and reading intervention programs, are the top-model predictor of improved high-stakes test scores, dropout rate reduction, course completion, and improved discipline. No other independent variable is the top-model predictor for more than one Education Success Measure.

This finding illustrates the power of the student-centric approach enabled by technology. In a setting in which each student works at his or her own pace, each student can take the time required to complete the course with demonstrated achievement. A few students will take longer than the traditional semester timeframe to complete the work, but not many.

Individualized instruction is perhaps the most important use model of technology in education. Whether advanced or remedial, individualized instruction allows students to learn at their own pace and engage in learning at exactly the right entry point. Technology-based learning solutions provide almost limitless opportunities for personalization. If one approach is not working for a student, alternatives can easily be tried that are better suited to a student's individual learning style or experiences. Because students are in active control of their learning, they are more likely to stay on task.

In the technology-transformed classroom, the teacher has more time for one-on-one instruction to address more difficult educational challenges. The effect of a technology transformation is similar to that of a class size reduction from 30 to 10 students, when measured by student–teacher face time.

Project RED data reveal that schools with 1-to-1 implementations tend to use technology frequently, across the entire range of subject areas, which is an indication that they may be experimenting with second-order change strategies enabled by the 1-to-1 student–computer ratio. By showing greater daily and weekly use of technology, the data suggest that the amount of time per subject per week is far greater in 1-to-1 schools than in others, which correlates to educational benefits. In addition, we find that 1-to-1 schools tend to encourage greater parental involvement, which is a key factor in student engagement.

This finding has significant financial implications. The improved course completion rate in technology-transformed interventions mitigates the direct cost of a repeated class, which is approximately $1,000 per student per class. Moreover, in schools with technology-transformed interventions, the repeat failure rate is far below the repeat failure rate of schools that re-teach in the traditional lecture mode.

The accompanying table shows the percentage of Project RED respondents reporting improvements in Education Success Measures from a technology deployment.

Technology-Transformed Intervention Classes Lead to Education Success

Education Success Measure (ESM)	Tech-Transformed Classes Daily (%)	All Other Schools (%)
Increase: High-stakes test scores	81	65
Reduction: Disciplinary action	63	51
Reduction: Dropout rate	59	45

Source: Project RED (www.projectred.org)

Online collaboration increases learning productivity and student engagement.

Online collaboration contributes to improved graduation rates and other academic improvements.

Collaboration and interaction among students have long been viewed as important factors in improving student achievement. Indeed, a student's participation in study groups is a good predictor of success in college. In the past, collaboration and study groups were generally limited to face-to-face interactions, but with the advent of the Internet many new technology-based collaboration experiences exist. Students quickly adopt them to reach out to peers.

Many students say that if they are having trouble with a particular concept, they use technology-based collaboration to query a peer for help. Social media substantially enhances collaboration productivity because it erases the barriers of time, distance, and money. Collaboration conducted through technology can extend beyond an individual's immediate circle of friends to become a worldwide network that includes mentors, tutors, and experts. Rapid technological advances in the fields of hardware and collaborative and social media will no doubt expand the benefits and options for participation available to users.

The accompanying table shows the percentage of Project RED respondents reporting improvements in Education Success Measures from online collaboration.

Online Collaboration Increases Student Engagement

Education Success Measure (ESM)	Using Online Collaboration (%)	All Other Schools (%)
Reduction: Disciplinary action	69	47
Reduction: Dropout rate	62	42

Source: Project RED (www.projectred.org)

Daily use of technology delivers the best return on investment (ROI).

To realize the benefits of technology, schools must incorporate technology into teaching on a daily basis.

The daily use of technology in core curriculum classes correlates highly to Education Success Measures, and hence return on investment. Daily technology use is a top-five indicator of better discipline, better attendance, and increases in college attendance.

Conversely, if a student spends only 30 minutes a week on a computer, the maximum productivity benefit is less than 2%. If technology use is an afterthought in the classroom, then even daily use of it may not produce dramatic improvements in student achievement, especially if students must constantly start, stop, and reacquaint themselves with the technology. Ultimately, schools that embed technology produce results in student achievement beyond those expected by chance.

In 1-to-1 schools—schools where every student has a computing device—daily use of technology in core curriculum classes ranges from 51% to 63%. Unfortunately, many 1-to-1 schools report using technology on a weekly basis, or less often, for many classes. Moreover, 40% of 1-to-1 schools report that students do not use technology on a daily basis. This is a surprising finding, but anecdotal evidence suggests a few reasons for it:

- Some schools move to 1-to-1 computing by way of top-down directives. These schools do not have critical stakeholder buy-in.

- Many schools do not have adequate levels of professional development.

- Schools buy the hardware but no courseware. In one large-scale implementation, the hardware vendor that won the bid allocated only 50 cents per machine per software application, which required the schools to purchase supplemental software.

- The laptops are used for less transformative activities. For example, students may be asked to use their computers to view a single website and then write a two-page report by hand on lined paper.

- Computer use is limited to tool use, such as presentation or word-processing applications, with some limited web browsing. Broader educational uses that include meaningfully integrated digital content are not employed.

Again, proper implementation (see Chapter 3) is the foundation for successfully deploying technology in schools, regardless of student–computer ratio. In the next chapter we will discuss the Education Success Measures that Project RED focused on and the Key Implementation Factors that were revealed to us by our research.

Project RED Education Success Measures and Key Implementation Factors

We launched Project RED because we were curious. As you know, the success or failure of a school program can be determined in numerous ways. Test scores are important, but they are only one measure of success. The Project RED team analyzed more than 4,000 pages of reports and evaluations from technology-rich implementations, primarily from 1-to-1 programs, and found little commonality in the success factors measured by schools.

Lacking a national consensus, the Project RED team chose 11 Education Success Measures (ESMs) that we believe provide a balanced view. These 11 ESMs were selected in order to elicit the most valuable information with the fewest number of variables. This filter eliminated many "nice-to-know" variables, such as student attendance. The measures were divided into two groups, those that affect students in all grades and those that affect students in high schools.

ESMs That Affect Students in All Grades

1. **Disciplinary action rate.** The frequency of disciplinary actions is a strong, leading indicator of academic success or failure. Fewer disciplinary actions mean that students are more likely to be engaged in learning. Also, every disciplinary action costs time and money.

2. **Dropout rate.** Dropouts are an extreme indicator of the lack of academic success and lead to high personal and societal costs.

3. **High-stakes test scores.** Any school improvement program needs to have a focus in this area.

4. **Paper and copying expenses.** This factor is a proxy for other similar school expense centers. Paper and copying machine expenses are more significant than often realized, particularly when labor is included.

5. **Paperwork reduction.** This factor is a proxy for efficiency savings attributable to technology. When paperwork is reduced, teachers have more time to spend on educationally productive tasks, and schools save other costs (such as storage and records retention).

6. **Teacher attendance.** Substitute teachers cost the district money and may impact student performance.

ESMs That Affect Students in High Schools

7. **AP course enrollment.** This factor indicates the quality of curriculum and instruction and reduces the time required to graduate from college, saving money for the state and for families.

8. **College attendance plans.** This factor indicates the quality of curriculum and instruction and facilitates students' educational planning.

9. **Course completion rates.** This factor indicates student engagement, achievement, and school quality. Conversely, course failure has severe negative academic and financial implications.

10. **Dual/joint enrollment in college.** This factor indicates a high level of student achievement and savings in future college expenses. The state saves money in subsidies for higher education and starts receiving tax revenues earlier.

11. **Graduation rates.** This factor indicates school quality and effective curriculum, instruction, and student planning. Multiple indicators, such as graduation and course completion rates, allow for better triangulation on a self-reported survey.

So, now that we have identified our ESMs, let's look at what leads to increased ESM scores.

We have said, more than once, that properly implemented educational technology leads to improved student outcome as well as cost savings. Now we'd like to define what we mean by "properly implemented." Following are, in order of predictive strength, the Project RED Key Implementation Factors, which correlate with success (ESMs).

1. **Intervention classes.** Technology is integrated into every intervention class period. Intervention classes include English language learners, Title I, special education, and reading intervention programs.

2. **Change management leadership by principal.** Leaders provide time for teacher professional learning and professional collaboration at least monthly.

3. **Online collaboration.** Students use technology daily for online collaboration (games, simulations, and social media).

4. **Core subjects.** Technology is integrated into core curriculum weekly or more frequently.

5. **Online formative assessments.** Assessments are done at least weekly.

6. **Student–computer ratio.** Lower ratios improve outcomes.

7. **Virtual field trips.** Virtual trips are done at least monthly.

8. **Search engines.** Students use daily.

9. **Principal training.** Principals are trained to lead effective implementation. Principals must ensure teacher buy-in and model best practices.

Now that we've introduced you to the Project RED Key Implementation Factors, we expect you may be asking the following question: What do these factors look like in practice? We'd like to answer this question with four brief, yet compelling, narratives and one emerging example detailing real-world success. Then, in Chapter 4, we'll review an in-depth case study of yet another successful school district.

Joplin Schools, Joplin, Missouri

Following a devastating tornado on May 22, 2011, which destroyed five schools and left several others heavily damaged, the Joplin School District was faced with a long list of challenges. After the status of its students and their families, along with district employees, was confirmed, Superintendent C. J. Huff immediately recognized the need to restore normalcy throughout the community. With steadfast conviction, he committed to readying and opening schools by the originally scheduled start date of August 17, 2011.

Demographics

Joplin Schools is a mostly urban district with an enrollment of 7,241 students. The majority (63%) of its students are eligible for free or reduced price lunch. It has a minority enrollment of 17%. Before the tornado of May 22, Joplin Schools had an enrollment of 7,571 students and had been experiencing steady enrollment increases for the last several years. Leadership in this district is made up of the following individuals: C. J. Huff, superintendent; Angie Besendorfer, assistant superintendent; and Traci House, director of technology.

In Record Time: 21st-Century Personalized Learning

To meet the start date, the district had to secure facilities to accommodate more than 3,500 students. Competition to secure properties was fierce, and Assistant Superintendent Besendorfer had to become an expert in the field of real estate nego-tiation. With great celebration, the district signed the necessary leases. The largest site was located in a vacant store at the Joplin mall.

The next decision, however, forever charted a new course of education for the students of Joplin School District. Two of the destroyed schools contained the bulk of the district's computers and other technology. Moreover, all textbooks for Grades 9–12 had been destroyed. Although this was a huge disaster, the leaders of Joplin schools recognized that this was an opportunity for the district to fast-forward its plans for creating a 21st-century learning environment.

District leaders chose not to replace numerous computer labs or classrooms that previously had provided computers in a 2-to-1 student-to-computer ratio. Instead, with the help of funds donated from the United Arab Emirates, leaders seized the opportunity to implement a 1-to-1 initiative for all 2,200 high school students. The district was fortunate in that it had previously developed a 21st-century vision team that included school staff, board members, university representatives, students, parents, and members of the business community. This team had visited many districts to gather information about forward-thinking philosophies and 21st-century practices, taking detailed notes about the measure of successes and disappointments these districts had experienced. The direct and indirect benefits of the insights gained during these visits provided to be immeasurable, because a successful implementation of the 1-to-1 initiative had to occur within 55 days. The severity of this challenge was magnified because the district's network infrastructure had to be rebuilt as a result of crushed fiber optics throughout the city of Joplin.

Even with these challenges, district and vision team leaders knew much more could be accomplished. Yet again these leaders transformed this disaster into an opportunity by implementing a personalized learning program with an open source curriculum, combined with access to 24/7 learning tools for all students.

Fortunately, in 2004 the district had implemented the Technology Leadership Academy, a program that required every teacher to complete 60 hours of professional development to receive a laptop. These educators could also have an interactive whiteboard and projector placed in their classrooms. In addition, the district-wide implementation of eMints, a model of high-impact technology embedded in the classroom, had mandated the incorporation of a 2-to-1 student to computer ratio. While many types of devices (various laptops, iPads, and other tablets) were considered for the new 1-to-1 initiative, teachers' familiarity with existing technology factored significantly in the selection criteria. Leaders of Joplin schools wanted the focus of the 1-to-1 initiative to be on pedagogy and, because of the time frame, a gradual learning curve for understanding new types of hardware was not possible.

Nonetheless, the leaders of Joplin School District were acutely aware that high-impact professional development for teachers would be critical to the success of the new personalized learning innovations. Department leaders reached out to multiple resources for guidance and assistance. Countless conference calls, videoconferences, and on-site visits involved experts not only from the K–12 pedagogy environment such as McREL, ICLE, and Leadership & Learning, but from the global market community as well, including Microsoft, Dell, Apple, Blackboard, and Hewlett Packard. The leaders of Joplin schools were extremely grateful for the compassion exhibited by everyone involved, as all were cognizant of the limited timeline and urgency with which the school district was working.

Armed with a wealth of information and resources, the leaders developed a curriculum that revolved around personalized learning for each student. Although the district had previously employed nine technology specialists and nine teaching and learning coaches, the Joplin school board was sensitive to the broad scope of change and the challenge of implementation. Without hesitation, the board approved the hiring of five additional 21st-century learning coaches to help guide and foster teachers, and together these professionals took the step forward to making Joplin's next vision a reality. A truly student-centered learning experience emerged. Collaboration, project-based learning, and constructivist pedagogy practices increased exponentially.

It would be doing a great disservice to any reader for Joplin Schools to claim they have experienced nothing but smooth sailing since the implementation of this initiative. As with any drastic change (and readers would be hard pressed to find a more disruptive education experience than what befell Joplin schools), the district has had its share of challenges and obstacles. The educators did not view any of these complications as a setback—instead, they learned, grew, and thrived with each experience. From the tragic events of May 22, Joplin Schools found a silver lining and ran with it. Has it been chaotic for them? Absolutely. Did they do the right thing? Without a doubt. Why? Because, they will tell you, what they did was best for their kids.

Office Hours in a 1-to-1 Classroom

Dustin Dixon, a social studies teacher at Joplin High School, knew that good teachers provide students with opportunities to receive additional assistance both during and outside of school. That is why he came to school early every morning and held tutoring sessions with anyone that might need extra support. After seeing the same lone student every morning, he realized that something needed to change: grades and missing assignments reflected a performance gap, but students were not taking the initiative to attend his tutoring sessions.

With the recent implementation of a 1-to-1 laptop distribution at the high school, Dixon seized an opportunity not previously available to him or his students. The evening before a test, Dixon announced to each of his sophomore classes that, starting at 9 p.m., he would log on to Skype, which was installed on every student computer in the 1-to-1 environment. He provided his username to students and offered online tutoring to anyone who might need help in preparing for the next day's test.

This caught students' attention. Their teacher was willing to meet them where they were—wherever that might be. That night, 34 students logged into Skype and received tutoring from their teacher. Sipping on coffee in the comfort of his own home, Dixon happily spent two hours working with his students. He provided information about make-up assignments, accepted assignments, and answered questions. This learning experience would have been impossible without the laptops that all students take home every night. Because of this success, Dixon continues to hold virtual office hours for students using Skype.

Sunnyside Unified School District, Tucson, Arizona— An Emerging Example

Sunnyside Unified School District (SUSD) launched Project Graduation in November, 2007. It is a multistrand, research-based effort to improve the graduation rate and ensure that all students have every opportunity to complete high school requirements and maintain the necessary credits toward graduation. Six strands create the framework for Project Graduation: site-based graduation plans for every student, credit recovery, freshman intervention, attendance monitoring, individualized advisory, and the Digital Advantage program.

The Digital Advantage program uses laptops as an incentive to impact student success by changing the culture. This technology-enhanced approach focuses on the four As: academics, attendance, activity, and attitude. For four years of the program (2008–11), SUSD awarded a netbook to every ninth-grade student who achieved the four A's at the end of the first semester:

- 95% attendance rate;

- 2.5 or higher grade point average;

- Participation in at least one extracurricular activity; and

- Good citizenship (no out-of-school suspensions).

The initiative captured the imaginations of business and community members who became partners in working toward the common causes of student success, family empowerment, and community progress. A total of 2,481 freshmen and upperclassmen earned netbooks over the four-year period. The partnership was inspired to move to a 1-to-1 computing model.

Demographics

Sunnyside Unified School District serves more than 17,800 students PK–12 in 22 schools. The district includes an early childhood education center, 13 elementary schools (Grades K–5), five middle schools (Grades 6–8), and three high schools (Grades 9–12) including one alternative education school. The district serves families with children from birth to five years of age, as well as PK–12 students. All SUSD schools have full-time counselors, registered nurses, music teachers, art teachers, physical education teachers, and librarians. The district is 94.4% minority students, with Hispanic ethnicity being the largest at 87.7%. Approximately 86% of SUSD students are eligible for free or reduced price lunch. About one-third of students are classified as English language learners. Approximately 14% of the district's student population receives Special Education services.

Moving toward 1-to-1 Computing

The success of the Digital Advantage program jumpstarted Sunnyside's transformation to the use of technology. The infusion of laptops into the classroom and community renewed both students' engagement in their own education and parents' visions of graduation and potential for college and careers for their children. The district is moving to 1-to-1 computing for the fifth grade in all 13 elementary schools and is planning to expand the 1-to-1 program into the sixth grade. The Sunnyside community affirmed the district's 1-to-1 mission with a successful bond vote in November 2011. This bond brings in additional technology dollars that will provide a foundation for 1-to-1 computing, first in Grades 4–9.

Sunnyside has placed a focus on research and professional learning to drive district-wide education technology decisions. New this past year is Sunnyside's plan to institute coaching staff to support technology integration in curriculum and instruction for 1-to-1 computing. The technology-coaching model is unique in that they have central technology coaches who mentor and train technology coaches at individual school. The goal is for classroom teachers to receive support in the daily integration of technology into lesson plans. This extended coaching model aims to build capacity on all levels, from curriculum design to lesson implementation.

Collaboration is a key component of teaching and learning on all levels at Sunnyside. Collaboration among teachers, between teachers and students, and among students is enhanced with anywhere-anytime 1-to-1 computing and access to the district's Moodle learning system. Early in the 2011 school year, a fifth-grade 1-to-1 classroom teacher had to spend time in a hospital bed but did not let the physical separation from his students limit his continued engagement with them and their school work. This program allowed him to communicate and collaborate with his students, and even advise on homework assignments, via the Moodle system. The Sunnyside Moodle learning system also allows for online sharing of lesson plans, formative assessments, and course development that is aligned to the Common Core State Standards (CCSS).

With the addition of purchased digital resources and free Internet resources, students have a rich digital library that is incorporated into their daily learning. Technology-based interventions are used liberally in Sunnyside's literacy model. Programs such as Reading Plus, Lexia, and DynEd provide a broad spectrum of learning opportunity for their English language learners and below–grade-level students.

But online learning goes beyond the classroom at Sunnyside. Many of the students' families are primary-language Spanish speakers who struggle in their quest to learn English. While students can work on vocabulary, fluency, comprehension, and phonics at school, the 1-to-1 laptops go home at the end of the day. This allows entire families to take advantage of the technology-based interventions enjoyed by students.

Sunnyside looks to operational efficiency and solid information technologies project management priorities to ensure success in deploying laptops into the hands of students. Placing a technician in every school and a technical assistant in each library has provided a foundation for technology support. These two technology support staff members are part of a larger 1-to-1 team at each school that includes the teacher technology coach, a parent-involvement assistant, and various instructional coaches.

Sunnyside's continuous review of program progess has led to several conclusions regarding the 1-to-1 program. Increased student engagement is the most visible and the obvious reason that Sunnyside has seen a reduction in disciplinary incidents, improved attendance, and academic progress. It is too early to credit changes in yearly state test scores to Sunnyside's 1-to-1 program. The district fortified its transition rate between fifth and sixth grade, and has kept kids in school where there was once a high level of loss from dropouts and transfer to other school districts or charter schools. In the two years since planning and early implementation of its 1-to-1 program, Sunnyside has seen open-enrolled students choosing to come to Sunnyside jump from 200 to 1,200 students.

Alvarado Independent School District, Alvarado, Texas

Alvarado began its classroom technology program in 2007. The district issued laptop computers to all students in Grades 4–6. Then, in 2009, the initiative evolved into a 1-to-1 program for students in Grades 7–8. The model was then rolled into the high school for Grades 9–12 with "a bring your own device" program. By the fall of 2012, the district plans to deploy a 1-to-1 computing solution to all students in

Grades 9–12. As of 2010, one third of the student population had a laptop computer; and 90% of all classrooms had mounted projectors, interactive whiteboards, and document cameras.

Demographics

Alvarado Independent School District (Alvarado ISD), a public school district based in Alvarado, Texas, also serves the unincorporated community of Lillian. The district spreads across 96 square miles and comprises six campus locations that serve 3,400 students, 70% of whom are economically disadvantaged.

Technology Integration Beginning at the Elementary Level

Because proper implementation is a critical component for the long-term success of a 1-to-1 computing technology initiative, Alvarado ISD spent three years laying the foundation for its program before phasing in its technology initiative.

During the first year of the program, the district streamlined the technology business process (account creation and management between systems). In the second year, the district started to expand its wireless network across the district and implemented sets of 24 laptops for every fourth grade classroom. In the third year, the district expanded its instructional technology department; finished the district-wide wireless expansion; established self-maintained and HP-certified technical staff; and expanded classroom laptop implementation to its second and third grade classrooms.

Thus prepared, when the fourth grade students reached the fifth grade, the district rolled out more than 750 laptops to all fifth and sixth grade classrooms. Each student was assigned a laptop that he or she could take from class to class (this model followed students into the sixth grade). In the meantime, the district finalized its technology take-home procedures; established and refined classroom and campus management plans; deployed specialized software to expand management and collaboration; and conducted intensive training programs for staff.

Thus, after three years of implementation all students in Grades 4–6 were using laptop computers. These devices were netbook-type computers, provided by HP. When these students reached the seventh grade, they were issued business-class notebooks, also provided by HP. These devices allow for 24/7 access, which enables students to access the Internet and perform schoolwork from remote locations. Students in Alvarado ISD use these devices through the eighth grade.

This phased approach, which Alvarado ISD dubs a "building responsibility" program, provides a meaningful and measured process that allows students to take "ownership" of the devices assigned to them. This approach proved to be very successful. During the four years of the program, only seven machines were lost or stolen; and of those seven machines four were recovered using Computrace software.

C.L.I.C.K.: Solving the Problem of Internet Access

Leaders of the Alvarado ISD technology initiative discovered that even though they could provide all students with a laptop, not all students or their families could afford Internet access in their homes. Likewise, the district could not afford to subsidize every family in need.

To meet this need, Kyle Berger, then executive director of technology at Alvarado ISD, developed a C.L.I.C.K. program (Community Located Internet Connected Kiosk) that provided free Internet hotspots to members of a given community.

The district placed these Alvarado ISD kiosks throughout the community, in fast food locations, churches, movie theaters, and even courthouse lobbies. Students of the Alvarado ISD merely had to find an Alvarado ISD kiosk to get online. Berger funded his district's C.L.I.C.K. program, which was powered by HP and Verizon Wireless, through advertising. The result was a zero-cost solution for both students and the district.

Starting in Fourth Grade

District leaders chose to begin the technology program at the fourth grade level for a number of important reasons: the technology would thoroughly engage students of this age, students in the program could be tracked for a long period of time, and the district could generate long-term support for this program in the larger community. Indeed, district leaders feared that if they began this program at the high school level they would run into difficultly when trying to convince the larger community to support the purchase of technology for the lower grades. Simply, district leaders wanted to prevent community members from thinking that technology was something that students "grew into" when they reached high school.

The district's plans worked. Because they introduced their technology program to the lower grades first, the community's involvement and support for the technology initiative grew along with the program itself. Parents and students who had experienced a 1-to-1 program at the elementary level wanted to continue that experience into middle school.

Leadership played a key role in all areas of the implementation plan and the overall policies that govern and administer the program. This technology program has produced a marked increase of technology integration into classroom learning, and has allowed the district to expand its distance learning programs. As well, the district reports a decrease in disciplinary problems.

Auburn City Schools, Auburn, Alabama

In 2006 Auburn City Schools launched its 21st Century Learning Initiative, a 1-to-1 program with a stated goal to "prepare … students and educators to be contributing members of an ever-increasing technological and global society through an anytime, anywhere learning environment." This program was successfully implemented at Auburn Junior High School. The program placed convertible tablets into the hands of all students in Grades 8–9, regardless of academic placement or ability level. The program was implemented in all core content areas as well as art and music.

While continuous support and wrap-around professional development remain imperative to the sustainability of this endeavor, program leaders and supporters are confident that through these resources and tools their students are better prepared and more adequately equipped to succeed in our constantly changing world.

Demographics

Auburn Junior High School in Auburn, Alabama, serves 1,065 students in Grades 8–9. The school consists of eight separate buildings that span a city block. The original building was constructed in 1931 and has served a variety of grade-level configurations over the years. The school's physical structures contains two gymnasiums, an auditorium, a cafeteria, a fine arts facility, a media center, an ACCESS learning lab, and 85 classrooms. The student demographic is: 60% Caucasian, 30% African-American, 7.2% Asian, and 2.8% Other; 27.32% of students qualify for free and reduced price lunch.

Auburn City Schools, serving 6,990 students, comprises 10 separate campuses: one kindergarten school, six elementary schools (Grades 1–5), one middle school (Grades 6–7), one junior high school (Grades 8–9), and one high school (Grades 10–12). Leadership consists of J. Terry Jenkins, superintendent, and Debbie B. Rice, director of technology.

Auburn City Schools spends $8,774 per student each year. All schools (Grades 1–12) have a media center, art teacher, music teacher, and one or more full-time counselors.

More than 67.54% of Auburn City Schools teachers and administrators hold advanced degrees; of these 20 have earned doctorates and three are pursuing doctoral degrees. The Board of Education is committed to keeping Auburn teachers' salaries in the top 10% in the state. They are currently ranked fourth. The overall pupil–teacher ratio in academic classes is 23-to-1; for Grades K–3, the pupil-teacher ratio is 18-to-1.

Measures of Success: The 21st Century Learning Initiative

Parent and community support and involvement is extremely strong at Auburn Junior High School. Parents are a vital part of improvement efforts at the school, and school leaders believe strongly in validating the voice of their stakeholders, and most importantly, their students. Auburn Junior High feels privileged to offer its students a rigorous academic program that is supported by technology. This support carries into the high schools, where students have earned many achievement awards in both academics and the arts. These achievements are realized through the Auburn City Schools 21st Century Learning Initiative. This program has three stated goals and a number of objectives for each:

Goal 1. Change and improve the delivery of instruction to realize the benefits of a 1-to-1 computing environment.

> *Objective 1.* Infuse curriculum, instructional methods, content, projects and lessons with 21st-century education technology throughout the daily delivery of classroom instruction.

> *Objective 2.* The learning environment will support Objective 1.

> *Objective 3.* The staff will have the skills and knowledge to achieve Objective 1.

Goal 2. Increase student achievement, engagement, and ability to learn to meet the demands of the world students are entering.

> *Objective 1.* Find the inherent and unique advantages of a 1-to-1 computing environment to increase student achievement, engagement (involvement, perseverance, effort, and attitude), and ability to learn.

> *Objective 2.* Utilize an appropriate mix of educational strategies.

> *Objective 3.* Use technology to assess student achievement, engagement, and learning ability levels, and respond appropriately.

> *Objective 4.* Motivate students to seek learning opportunities to use technology as an extension of the classroom.

Goal 3. Create and support equitable opportunities for student learning through the use of technology as an extension of the classroom.

> *Objective 1.* Students will know how to properly use the technology as an extension of the classroom.

> *Objective 2.* The school system will achieve a 1-to-1 student–computer ratio beyond the classroom for Grades 9–12.

> *Objective 3.* Ensure all students in Grades 9–12 have Internet access from home.

Teachers and administrators at Auburn City Schools spent a year of preparation prior to initiating the 1-to-1 program. They studied other school districts, mapped out a 10-year budget, assessed the readiness of staff, conducted professional development programs, selected appropriate technologies, and collaborated with parents and community members. As a result, Auburn City Schools has experienced distinct improvements that can, in large part, be attributed to the successful implementation of its 1-to-1 computing program.

High-Stakes Test Scores

Auburn City Schools has consistently made annual yearly progress (AYP) every year since 2004.

Paper and Copying Expenses, Paperwork Reduction

The technology system at Auburn incorporates the Moodle Learning System, which provides assignment submissions, discussion forums, file downloads, and more. A parent portal system is used for grade reporting, teacher web pages, and phone call-outs for announcements and school-related activity updates. Training documentation is typically posted on websites or through flash drives to reduce printing of documentation. Data is stored on shared storage spaces for collaborative access when needed. The result is a more timely distribution of information and a measurable reduction of paperwork.

AP Course Enrollment

The number of AP/IB exams given for high school students has been consistent. The exams are administered online, and the number of students who have passed the exams and qualified for awards and recognitions increases each year.

College Attendance Plans

Auburn High School has hired a staff member whose responsibility is enhancing the college application, financial aid, and scholarship practices of seniors. Because the high school counselors have consistent and accurate access to student information, they are able to effectively meet with students and parent groups to determine career paths, class placement, and curriculum planning.

Dual/Joint Enrollment in College

Dual enrollment for Auburn High School is restricted to six students per semester per year, which equates to a possibility of 24 students per year. The program enrolled 11 students in 2010–11 and nine students in 2011–12. Students use ACCESS, a statewide distance learning initiative that provides high-quality classroom courses and teachers via technology to students, allowing them to progress at their own pace.

Graduation Rates

The Alabama State Department of Education provides an accountability web portal that allows access to state testing information and reporting for K–12 students in Alabama. Through this portal, all school districts have access to student account-ability information such as graduation rate, AYP information, and SAT testing information. This trend data allows the district to compare schools and school systems throughout the state, which then allows Auburn City Schools to identify additional areas for improvement. In 2009–10, the graduation rate was 96%; in 2010–11, the graduation rate was 97.21%.

Klein Independent School District, Klein, Texas

The success of Klein Independent School District (Klein ISD) is rooted in a unified vision of technology's role in supporting student success. This vision is combined with a strong and ongoing job-embedded professional development program and visionary leadership within all curriculum, student support, and campus administration areas.

Demographics

Klein ISD is fully accredited by the Texas Education Agency and the Southern Association of Colleges and Schools. Located near Houston, Texas, Klein ISD has 6,000 employees who serve a highly diverse district of 46,000 students. The district covers 87.5 square miles of north Harris County and comprises 27 elementary schools, nine intermediate schools, and four high schools. The district ethnicity is 0.4% American Indian, 8.3% Asian, 13.8% Black-American, 35.9% Hispanic, 0.2% Native Hawaiian, 2.7% Two or More, and 38.7% White. Ann McMullan is executive director for educational technology.

Klein ISD Technology Initiatives

Launched in 2004, the district's Technology Baseline Standard Initiative (TBSI) assures that all students have ready access to a suite of technology tools for learning in their classrooms. In addition, teachers are prepared to maximize those tools through the implementation of an updated curriculum. Today, every core content classroom in Grades K–12 has an interactive whiteboard, a classroom assessment "clicker" system, a projector, a document camera, and a minimum of four networked computers for students and a teacher computer, all complete with a full complement of software productivity tools and access to hundreds of online interactive learning resources. The combination of powerful learning tools, leadership at all levels, and teachers who are committed to making it all work—through research-based instructional strategies—has produced learning innovations across the entire school district.

Recognizing that 24/7 access to powerful productivity tools and digital resources is key to any 21st-century learning program, Klein ISD launched a 1-to-1 tablet PC program in 2006. To date, more than 8,600 students at four school locations have been issued tablet PC computers as part of the district's 1-to-1 student computer initiative.

The decision to provide students with tablet PCs is rooted in the district's strategic plan, which was the result of months of research and collaborative work by a visioning committee comprising community members, parents, district and campus administrators, teachers, and students. The visioning committee used the Texas *Long Range Plan for Technology 2006–2020* as a guide. In addition, the district's mission statement articulates a commitment to embrace the future and to provide engaging learning experiences for all students. To meet the district's goals, it was determined that providing Klein ISD students with 24/7 access to digital instructional materials and productivity tools would take place through a planned roll-out program, adding one school per year.

Technical Preparations for Going 1-to-1

Before embarking on a 1-to-1 initiative at any of its schools, Klein ISD had to make sure that the infrastructure and technical support would be in place to assure that students had daily access to the programs that were to be provided to them through their 24/7 access to their tablet PCs. At each school, a robust wireless infrastructure was installed and a technical repair center was established so that students could have their tablet PCs fixed on site. Depending on the size of the school, one clerical assistant and either one or two full-time technicians were assigned to each campus technical repair center.

Professional Development and Instructional Support in a 1-to-1 School

A major objective for Klein ISD's 1-to-1 tablet PC program was to strategically change instructional practices for teachers and students. As such, a strong ongoing professional development program was developed to support the 1-to-1 program. Teachers at Klein ISD receive their tablet PCs one year before students are issued computers. One or two campus instructional technology specialists (depending on the size of the school) are hired the same year that the teachers receive their tablet PCs. These technology specialists lead and support the teachers in this change process. Professional development for teachers and administrators goes far beyond simply learning how to use the technology. Continued research and implementation of best practices around instructional strategies is at the core of the Klein ISD's year-round job-embedded professional development program. In addition to working with their campus instructional technology specialists, teachers work together in professional learning communities to support each other in this process.

Impact on Standardized Test Results: All Students

Though the success of any educational program can never be isolated to one factor or initiative, Klein ISD has some data that speaks to the impact of the 1-to-1 tablet PC program—combined with an updated curriculum and training in instructional strategies—as measured by the Texas Assessment of Knowledge and Skills (TAKS) test. The following table shows the changes in student performance on the TAKS test for two Klein ISD high schools that have the 1-to-1 tablet PC program. The scores in the year prior to the students receiving their tablet PCs are compared to the years after the students received tablet PCs.

Tracking TAKS Data Before and After 1-to-1 Program Initiation: All Students

	Klein Oak High School					Klein Forest High School				
	Students who met the standards (%)				Point gain (%)	Students who met the standards (%)				Point gain (%)
	Before 1-to-1	1st Year	2nd Year	3rd Year	Cumulative	Before 1-to-1	1st Year	2nd Year	Cumulative
Reading/ELA	90	92	94	93	3	85	89	87	2
Math	76	81	84	82	6	60	67	69	9
Science	78	86	90	91	13	69	79	81	12
Social Studies	92	95	97	98	6	91	93	95	4

Data Sources: TEA, KOHS AEIS Report, KFHS Campus Accountability Data Table, KFHS AEIS Report, KFHS Campus Accountability Data Table

Impact on Standardized Test Results: Economically Disadvantaged Students

When Klein ISD looks at the impact of 1-to-1 computing on its economically disadvantaged student population (which is now just over 40% for the district) the student gains immediately after the implementation of the 1-to-1 tablet PC program are even more impressive. Klein Oak High School (4,100 students) has 27% of it student body classified as economically disadvantaged. Klein Forest High School's student population (3,500 students) is 65 % economically disadvantaged.

Tracking TAKS Data Before and After 1-to-1 Program Initiation: Economically Disadvantaged Students

	Klein Oak High School					Klein Forest High School				
	Students who met the standards (%)				Point gain (%)	Students who met the standards (%)				Point gain (%)
	Before 1-to-1	1st Year	2nd Year	3rd Year	Cumulative	Before 1-to-1	1st Year	2nd Year	Cumulative
Reading/ELA	78	82	90	89	11	83	87	85	2
Math	59	65	73	69	10	57	64	68	11
Science	58	71	81	82	24	65	76	79	14
Social Studies	81	88	92	95	14	89	92	94	5

Data Sources: TEA, KOHS AEIS Report, KFHS Campus Accountability Data Table, KFHS AEIS Report, KFHS Campus Accountability Data Table

Final Thoughts

As leaders at Klein ISD reflect on the reasons for launching their instructional technology initiatives, they see that their goals of embracing the future and engaging students in their learning are being met. Having moved forward with establishing an environment that is equipped and functional from both the infrastructure and instructional perspectives, Klein ISD is poised to move easily into the opportunities that the world of digital learning provides.

As textbooks move from print to digital format, Klein ISD is ready to embrace them. Student products that demonstrate their learning of content standards are also moving from print to digital format, and students are sharing their products well beyond their classroom walls. Putting a priority on technology for learning—combined with a robust, rigorous curriculum and professional development that is focused on effective instructional strategies—has allowed Klein ISD to align its curriculum to college and career readiness standards and implement best practices for mastery of vital 21st-century skills that include critical thinking, communication, collaboration, and creativity.

Conclusion

We hope you were inspired by these snapshots of real-world success! These districts followed many of our Key Implementation Factors and reaped the benefits.

The Project RED Key Implementation Factors encompass several important aspects of instruction that contribute to improved achievement. When every student has a personal portable computing device connected to the Internet, the opportunity for students to work independently and at their own pace dramatically increases, along with the opportunity for teachers to address the individual needs of each student. Ongoing instant feedback provides the data to make important individualized adjustments to the instructional process. Social media, games, simulations, and virtual field trips engage students in the learning process. And when technology is integrated into every intervention class and into the daily core curriculum, students and teachers have the opportunity to practice and improve their skills on an ongoing basis. Keep these nine factors in mind as you continue through the chapters ahead.

CHAPTER 4

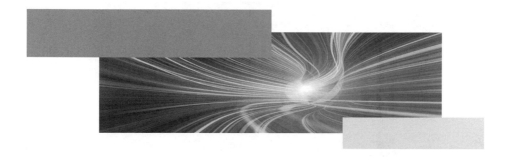

Case Study: Mooresville Graded School District

Mooresville, North Carolina, is a blue-collar former mill town in suburban Charlotte. Affectionately known as "Race City, USA," Mooresville is home to several NASCAR teams, the NASCAR Institute of Technology, and the national headquarters for Lowe's Home Improvement.

In the fall of 2007, the Mooresville Graded School District launched a digital conversion campaign. The real-world purpose, process, and results of its efforts provide a model for other schools to follow.

Demographics: Mooresville Graded School District, Mooresville, North Carolina

Schools	8
Students	5,409
Poverty	39% free and reduced price lunch (up from 31% in 2006–07)
Ethnicity	73% Caucasian, 15% African-American, 7% Hispanic, 3% Multiracial, 2% Asian

Source: Project RED (www.projectred.org)

Background

In the 2006–07 school year, Mooresville Graded School District conducted an in-depth review of district results in teaching and learning. A new superintendent, Mark Edwards, who had pioneered the use of a digital environment in Henrico County, Virginia, was on board. This review of test scores and other Education Success Measures by the leadership team revealed results that were acceptable but not leading edge. A decision was made to transform the school district into one of high achievement, both within the state and nationally.

To achieve this goal, the team looked at how students learned and considered how to engage them at a higher level. The resulting "Digital Conversion" project was launched in fall 2007. Although technology was seen as the tool, the driving force behind this initiative was a desire to provide more relevant content and tools to engage students. The objectives were multifaceted:

- **Close the digital divide.** While one-third of students qualified for free and reduced price lunch, many others were from affluent homes and had their own computing devices.

- **Provide relevant instruction.** Students were used to accessing information quickly at home; at school they often encountered out-of-date information in static formats.

- **Ensure 21st-century readiness.** Students needed the skills necessary to function in an increasingly connected and collaborative world.

- **Create real-world experiences.** Students needed to work with one another as work teams do and learn how to work cooperatively.

- **Use best instructional practices.** Research shows that students who construct meaning learn far better than those who just absorb facts from others.

- **Improve academic achievement.** The hypothesis was that the goal of improving learning might also lead to significant gains in test scores.

So the planning began. Through research and personal experience, the team knew that teacher empowerment and community buy-in were essential characteristics, and they included those elements in the plan.

Implementation: December 2007–August 2010

The rollout of laptops was phased to ensure a smooth transition and working environment.

- **December 2007.** Every teacher in the district received a laptop. (Note, this is a Project RED best practice: Giving devices first to teachers, and later to students, ensures they maintain control of their own learning and can develop integrative practices for teaching on a developmental basis.)

- **January 2008.** Professional development began, followed by a summer institute for faculty in July 2008.

- **August 2008.** Laptops were distributed to all students in Mooresville High School and Mooresville Intermediate School. Interactive whiteboards were installed in all K–2 classrooms at Parkview and South Elementary Schools.

- **November 2008–June 2009.** Phased distribution of laptops to students at other district schools began.

- **July 2009.** A second summer institute took place with more than 300 teachers in attendance.

- **August 2009.** At this point every student in Grades 4–12 had a laptop to use at both school and home, and every student in Grades K–3 was in a classroom equipped with an interactive whiteboard.

- **July 2010.** The third summer institute took place, with continuing refinement of professional development and integration of technology into the curriculum.

- **December 2010.** Mooresville Graded School District viewed the initiative as one of continuing movement toward adaptation and adoption.

The Results

In 2009–10, Mooresville was one of only six districts in North Carolina that made all of their adequate yearly progress (AYP) targets, and Mooresville had the highest number of targets met. All schools in the district were recognized in 2009–10 as Schools of Distinction. Rocky River Elementary School was recognized as an Honor School of Excellence by the state. The percentages in the following table represent students graded as proficient or higher on end-of-grade reading, math, and science tests.

North Carolina State Performance and Academic Composite Data

Year	Mooresville Graded School District (% of students graded proficient or higher)
2007–08	73%
2008–09	82% (ranked eighth in state)
2009–10	86% (tied for fourth in state while ranked 101 out of 115 in per-pupil expenditures)
2010–11	88% (tied for third in state while ranked 99 out of 115 in per-pupil expenditures)

Source: Mooresville School District

Aside from the impressive improvements in Education Success Measures, the results in Mooresville can be evaluated through the body language of the students, who lean forward into their laptops as they work. The hum in the schools' hallways is energetic. A visit to the schools, which have received more than 750 visitors from 150 districts from more than 25 states, is inspiring.

Technology has played a significant part in improving teaching and learning through increased student engagement in Mooresville classrooms. Laptop computers have significantly enhanced the level of student interest, motivation, and engagement to learn. The focus is to engage students with instructional tools, add value to their performance, and realize improved achievement in all aspects of their school experiences.

> We knew that our Digital Conversion project was the right move for students, teachers, and the community based on the need to create a relevant experience in our schools that will prepare students for their future.
>
> —Mark Edwards, EdD
> Superintendent, Mooresville Graded School District

Out-of-school suspensions have decreased by 64% since 2006–07, and the go-to-college rate has increased from 74% to 75% since 2006–07.

Mooresville Graded School District had the highest 2010 graduation rate when compared with other districts in the Charlotte region and the three largest districts in North Carolina. (The numbers reflect the percentage of students who started ninth grade in 2006–07 and graduated by 2010.) The graduation rate was highest for every subset, including ethnicity, low income, disabled, and limited English proficient.

As one of the lowest expenditure per-student districts in the state (101 out of 115 districts), Mooresville continues to look for economies from its Digital Conversion initiative. As the district moves into this digital world, the need for traditional tools like textbooks continues to wane. As a result, Mooresville has redistributed funds to help fund the Digital Conversion project.

Modeling the business environment, students now work around tables with their laptops instead of at individual desks. This change has saved approximately 20% on furniture costs. Additional cost savings have resulted from embedded graphing calculators and online access to maps, three-dimensional globes, dictionaries, libraries, thesauruses, and publications.

Conclusion

We hope you found the case study of the Mooresville Graded School District's Digital Conversion project illuminating. We believe it is evidence that a technology implementation done according to best practices will yield high student achievement and cost savings. And Mooresville is just one success story. There are many more out there!

CHAPTER 5

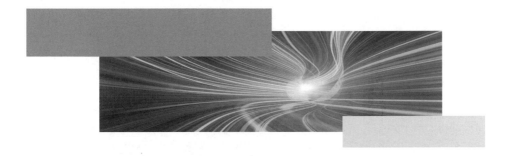

The Importance of School Leadership

Strong school-level leadership is essential to the success of a technology initiative. To properly implement technology in our schools, education leaders and policymakers at all levels must have an understanding of technology use from the perspective of school-level leadership. For these reasons, Project RED focused on the contribution made by principals and other leaders at the school level.

In this chapter we discuss the role of school leadership in successful educational technology implementations. We focus on and provide recommendations for four areas: instruction, cost savings, policy, and industry. For a deep dive into the data that led us to these recommendations, please refer to our full report, *The Technology Factor: Nine Keys to Student Achievement and Cost-Effectiveness* (Greaves, Hayes, & One-to-One, 2010; available at www.projectred.org).

Instruction

The expectations of a school's principal drive student performance. Student motivation and engagement increase when students have consistent access to digital learning tools, and school-level leaders establish those access expectations for students. The relationship between students' use of technology tools and school leaders' expectations is consistent with the research that demonstrates the important role of leadership in improving student outcomes.

Another factor in improving student outcome is the accessibility and functionality of technology tools. Consistent access to the Internet exposes students to information for research, analysis, problem solving, and global and local connections. When integrated into teaching and learning, technology resources allow for productivity in knowledge access, evaluation, and real-time content aligned with standards. Gaming and simulation solutions are increasingly higher quality, tied to real-life issues, and require higher-order thinking and skill sets.

Ongoing professional development for school leaders is essential for successful technology initiatives. Leading a technology-transformed school calls for different skills from those needed in a traditional Industrial-age school. To set expectations and provide support, leaders must develop insights and skills related to first- and second-order change so that robustly infused technology can create a teaching and learning environment that is dynamic, systematic, and natural. When school leaders facilitate second-order change, systems become organic—possibilities and discoveries replace right and wrong answers. Students need guided practice in media and Internet literacy, which calls for agility, flexibility, trial and error, and up-front planning on the part of educators. Leadership in all of these areas is key to successful technology-transformed classrooms.

Teachers must continually hone their ability to create and improve the 21st-century computer-enhanced learning environment. Professional learning is essential for teacher growth in terms of effectively integrating education technology. Commitment and high expectations from principals are mirrored by teachers, which leads to increased student success.

The Importance of Teacher Training

It is generally accepted that teachers should receive technology and training before technology is released to students. Teachers need time to become familiar with the equipment, operating systems, and tools, and to review the various resources that work with their lessons and state standards. Many experts suggest an interval of three to six months, with six or more months preferred.

Several components lead to success in this area, including the following:

- **Service and support.** Student and teacher laptops must be available 100% of the time. If it takes more than 30 minutes to repair or replace a device, the teacher's ability to deliver instruction is hindered.

- **Instructional network.** The network must be robust. It must support log-on and vigorous activity by every student at the same time.

- **Teacher buy-in and training.** If teachers are not engaged, they generally do not buy in to a technology initiative. If they do not buy in, they generally do not take advantage of professional development opportunities or modify their teaching behavior to accommodate and exploit technology.

- **Long-term funding.** Adequate funding is required to sustain a technology initiative. When funding is in jeopardy, teachers and administrators tend to withdraw from the program and start planning for life after technology. A large number of 1-to-1 implementations have failed when the hardware aged and the money ran out.

- **Parent/guardian involvement.** Parental involvement and high expectations lead to more time on task and affect student achievement. Also, fully involving parents can reduce the number of lost, stolen, and damaged devices.

Professional Learning Activities for Teachers

Professional learning (also called professional development) has been the most frequently overlooked component of technology integration since schools began using technology. As long ago as 2000, the U.S. Department of Education tried to set a model expectation by requiring that 25% of all EETT (Enhancing Education Through Technology) funds be set aside for professional development.

Education leaders must understand that to make professional learning an essential part of technology in instruction, more time must be spent on the activities identified in this section. For example, while schools with 1-to-1 student–computer ratios report a higher frequency of teacher training than schools with higher student–computer ratios, less than half of 1-to-1 schools report use of in-class mentoring at least weekly. Because in-class mentoring is one of the most effective kinds of professional learning, frequency as well as appropriate planning is critical.

It is well established that professional learning is crucial to teaching quality and enhanced student learning. A key component is combining new learning with on-the-job experience, reflection, and debriefing. Coaching and mentoring are ideal for adult learning because they fuel personal awareness through personalized reflection. Co-planning, collaborating, coaching, and debriefing are key elements for professional learning communities.

Teachers involved in these professional interactions are able to hone their skills by applying knowledge on the job, and then reflecting on and debriefing those experiences with colleagues. These teacher experiences translate to better classroom practices and highly informed instructional techniques, enhancing the opportunity for personalization.

Cost Savings

If principals expect frequent use of technology tools in the classroom, the expectation will ensure a return on the school's investment. When students and teachers use technology resources to communicate, teachers can respond more quickly to student needs and make appropriate instructional adjustments. Research and collaboration tools available on a just-in-time basis can expedite a more productive teaching and learning experience. These practices decrease the need for remediation.

The expanded use of digital resources reduces the need for hard-copy resources and textbooks. Digital subscriptions, open source software, games/simulations, and teacher- or student-created content all lead to budget savings. Consistent Internet access may require additional upfront resources, but the return on that investment is realized when leaders, teachers, and students move from static tools to dynamic Internet-based tools.

When teachers are performing at capacity, the result is improvements in student achievement, increases in matriculation, and fewer dropouts. The need to retrain and discipline ineffective teachers is reduced when every teacher is engaged in consistent learning opportunities. If teachers are meeting learner needs, there can be savings in remedial interventions, and teachers collaborating on student needs can reduce the need for costly special education referrals and services.

Professional learning that builds internal capacity rather than supporting episodic training events produces a tremendous return on investment. When teachers learn and grow together, the need for outside consultants disappears over time. Coaching, collaborating, and co-planning can be incorporated into a teacher's daily or weekly schedule using creative scheduling. High standards for teacher growth and a way to achieve those standards increase teacher productivity and the focus on instructional techniques.

Each of these elements reduces the costs of travel and substitutes that occur when teachers must leave the school building for professional development. Funds saved can be redeployed toward improving student achievement. Blending online professional development with face-to-face is highly cost-effective.

Policy

School leadership is a key factor for student achievement, and mandates for quality principal development are very helpful. University-level professional growth programs can ensure that theory becomes practice through robust internships, on-the-job coaching, and accreditation. These efforts must include a high level of educational technology theory and practice for both instructional and administrative purposes.

The world is moving from static to dynamic digital resources. Uninterrupted access to the Internet is imperative for a globally competitive education system. Educators, business, and industry will be well served if key decision makers push for resource allocation for last mile and infrastructure development that leads to consistent digital access. Of equal importance is professional training for educators on the effective integration of web-based resources into the curriculum and instructional programs.

Transformed school leadership is needed for school reform. Technology initiatives present new expectations and a shift from traditional to dynamic, self-discovered tools and resources. To effectively use these tools, school leaders need professional growth experiences that help them become nimble thinkers, skilled problem solvers, and confident facilitators of learner-centered models. They must also develop a keen understanding of each staff person's ability to embrace first- and second-order change. This is difficult work. It is easy to tinker at the edges without affecting the entire system, but only revamping the entire system leads to authentic school reform.

Education leadership programs need to support lifelong learning for administrators to make sure they can keep pace with the skills required for this century. National- and state-level policies should require that school leaders pursue ongoing leadership development and demonstrate their skills through supervised practicums. School boards and district administrators must standardize expectations and accountability systems to help leaders develop and practice effectiveness in today's schools. National, state, and local policies must set standards of leadership, accompanied by account-ability measures that ensure effective school transformation.

It is well established that educators need consistent, ongoing professional development in pedagogy, best practices, research, content, curriculum, and the personalization of instruction. We also know that educators learn best through the on-the-job application of best practices, reflection with peers, and collaboration on how to implement theories in the classroom. Effective school leaders provide ongoing, embedded professional development in order to ensure best practices for new century education. Federal, state, and local policies should support the expectation that principals will actively seek, develop, and implement robust professional learning for themselves and their teachers.

Increased internal capacity for building student achievement and teacher professional growth decreases external support costs. Virtual experiences are cost-effective, at minimum eliminating the costs of travel and substitutes. When educators become coaches and resources for each other, they begin to expect growth and use best practices, leading to increased student success.

Online professional learning will increasingly replace the need to travel to gain knowledge and skills. Online professional networks of best practices will increase just-in-time access to, as well as the exchange and application of, quality instruction, although ongoing face-to-face interaction will still be essential in certain situations. The power of getting people to sit down together to work on a problem cannot be underestimated.

Industry

The increased expectations of schools and the increased use of technology tools, gaming, and simulations present new opportunities for industry. As learning management systems and collaboration, communication, and gaming tools become integrated into daily teaching and learning, schools need user-friendly and age-appropriate tools. Tools that enhance elementary and middle school student collaboration, along with appropriate professional development, are especially needed. Learning platforms that incorporate these tools, and that can be easily integrated into existing infrastructures, will be attractive to schools.

Other than in the daily use of search engines, education is still in the embryonic stages of implementing robust technology instruments. This offers industry the opportunity to create user-friendly and grade-friendly instruments that incorporate technology tools, particularly collaboration and learning management systems based on research and best practices in the areas of personalization, formative assessment, and data-driven instruction. Schools will also be looking for the integration of quality professional development.

While organizational change theory has already been incorporated into business practice, it is just now emerging in education. Educators can learn best practices and strategies from business leaders and researchers to move their organizations forward. Industry can help unpack and adapt business practices so that they are relevant and user-friendly for educators and make the information available online.

Recent U.S. Department of Education research shows that the most effective instructional platform is a combination of face-to-face and online learning. Because schools have continual budget constraints, moving a large portion of the professional learning program to an online format makes economic sense. Industry has an opportunity to provide top-quality, cost-effective learning experiences that are accessible 24/7, with a moderator who provides ongoing direction and feedback. This combination is likely to become the leading mode of educator preparation and lifelong learning and positively affect higher education and teacher and administrator preparation programs. The more contemporary and innovative the program, the more likely that educators will gravitate to the experience.

Another opportunity for industry is to develop advanced collaboration and productivity tools for educators. More and more principals are providing time for teacher collaboration and interaction, with joint problem solving and other forms of productivity. Moving these activities to online, web-, and cloud-based systems will be the way of the future.

Conclusion

School leaders play an important role in ensuring quality instruction, professional learning, and student achievement. If a school principal expects students and teachers to use technology tools frequently, they will do so. Student motivation and engagement increases when students and teachers have consistent access to digital learning tools, and school-level leaders establish those access expectations for students.

CHAPTER 6

Technology and the School Environment

As of this writing, approximately 2% of schools in the United States have a 1-to-1 student–computer ratio. Project RED data reveal that schools with a 1-to-1 student–computer ratio outperform non–1-to-1 schools on both academic and financial measures. Significantly, Project RED data show that schools with a 2-to-1 student–computer ratio perform more like 3-to-1 schools than 1-to-1 schools.

In this chapter, we discuss the role of the school environment in successful educational technology implementations. We cover several different topics, and following a quick survey of each topic, we focus on and provide recommendations in four areas: instruction, cost savings, policy, and industry. For a deep dive into the data that led us to these recommendations, please refer to our website at www.projectred.org.

Frequency of Technology Use in Instruction

The behavior of teachers and students in 1-to-1 schools is considerably different from the behavior of teachers and students in schools with higher student–computer ratios. Students who have continuous access to a computing device clearly take more control of their own learning than students with infrequent access to a variety of different devices, where links and materials cannot be stored and exploration is limited.

- **Using a wide range of electronic materials.** 1-to-1 schools report 37 points higher frequency (83% vs. 46%) than schools with 4-to-1 or higher ratios.

- **Using problem-based learning.** 1-to-1 schools report 32 points higher frequency (75% vs. 43%) than schools with 4-to-1 or higher ratios.

- **Taking control of their own learning.** 1-to-1 schools report 35 points higher frequency (75% vs. 40%) than schools with 4-to-1 or higher ratios.

Some courses are better suited to technology use than others. Lower usage levels of technology in health and physical education are understandable. Likewise, higher usage levels of technology in courses such as math, social studies, and science is expected. Science and social studies, in particular, are changing on a daily basis, and the amount of information available online far surpasses in quantity and quality what is available in traditional textbooks.

Device Types

Continuous personal access to a computing device and the Internet dramatically expands the intellectual resources available to students and ensures a dynamic, rather than static, education setting. It is encouraging that many of the schools that reported higher than 1-to-1 student–computer ratios are finding ways to provide their students with high levels of access to technology.

At the time of our survey, mobile devices constituted 45% of the computing devices used in schools (laptops, netbooks, tablets, and smartphones). However, different implementation levels may limit the benefits of mobile computing. The Michigan Freedom to Learn program, for example, saw high levels of usage in English language arts, social studies, and science and low levels of usage in math. The tablet computer seems to hold promise for increasing student usage in math. The benefits seem to be equally shared by teachers and students, with the tablet computer providing a new level of freedom and interactive learning in the classroom. Since the Project RED survey was conducted, the iPad and Android-based tablets have found strong acceptance in schools among early adopters. Given inevitable advances in technology, iPad-type devices will only grow in popularity.

Nonetheless, education leaders must understand the following school-level realities. At 54% of total, desktops are the most prevalent device. The vast majority (95%) of respondents report that they have desktops in their environment. The highest percentage was found in elementary schools, with penetration of almost 98%, followed by high schools at 92% and middle schools at 90%—a different mix from computing devices (including laptops).

At 37% of total, computing devices are a fast-growing category in the schools of the Project RED respondents. A majority (91%) of respondents report that they have computing devices in their environment. The distribution is more weighted to secondary schools—94% of middle schools, 92% of high schools, and 88% of elementary schools. Only 5% of total devices reported are netbooks, with 13% of schools reporting some number of netbooks in their environment. The breakdown across grade levels is approximately 10% elementary schools, 10% middle schools, and 16% high schools.

Just over 2% of total devices reported are tablet computers, but the percentage of schools with some number of tablets is equal to that of netbooks at 13%. The breakdown across grade levels is approximately 8% of elementary schools, 13% of middle schools, and 15% of high schools. All but two respondents completed the survey before iPads were shipped, thus understating the tablet share.

Only 1% of total devices reported are smartphones, and 33 of the 144 schools that report having smartphones have only one such device. When subtracting respondents with only one or two smartphones, the implementation percentage remains in the low single digits across all grade levels.

Finally, only 1% of total devices reported are thin clients (a thin client is a computing device or software that depends on a server to operate). The breakdown for thin-client deployment across grade levels is evenly distributed—approximately 3% of elementary and middle schools and 4% of high schools.

Reliability of Instructional Network

A reliable network is essential in any digital learning environment. It is important that a school's network is never down for more than a few seconds, and that long periods of downtime are rare. If students and teachers become frustrated by unreliable access, they will soon stop using the network.

If technology does not work reliably, teachers and students will not use it. And if technology is not being used, it cannot contribute to student improvement. Providing informal technical support to students is estimated to be 10% of teacher time, which is taken out of instructional time. More teacher time on task equals better results. School administrators interviewed by the Project RED team believe that a reliability rate of 99.9% is required before schools can move from print to digital materials.

As schools make the switch from print to digital media, the speed of the Internet connection takes center stage. Many factors drive bandwidth needs, including the number of computers, usage patterns in the classroom, the types of materials accessed (e.g., email or video), and the intensity of access (e.g., a course or a Google search). Schools today are by and large under-provisioned, and the educational impact of insufficient bandwidth can be significant. If a student spends an hour a day on the Internet, with sufficient bandwidth the unproductive wait time could be reduced as much as 50%. Ten minutes saved during the school day is equivalent to five extra school days a year, and 30 minutes saved is equivalent to 15 days. Doubling the bandwidth costs roughly $12 per student per year. Providing five more instructional days would cost roughly $222 per student per year. Thus, we see that sufficient bandwidth is absolutely critical.

To be most useful, digital materials and resources must be available wherever print materials are currently being used—at school, at home, at the park, at the orthodontist's office, and other places. When teachers, students, and parents can access the instructional network anytime/anywhere, communication and information sharing are simplified. Moreover, full access to digital resources can lengthen the school day, and more student engagement in learning leads to improvements in outcomes.

Technology Implications for Instruction

Students who have anytime/anywhere access to the instructional network enjoy several advantages. Neither student nor parent has to trek back to school in the hope of finding a custodian who will let them retrieve a forgotten textbook. When students are sick, they can avoid falling behind by accessing lessons and resources from home. Students can also communicate with teachers as needed, helping to build the personal relationships that are known to be an important factor in student achievement.

With a couple of mouse clicks, teachers can send messages to all parents or private communications to individual parents and students. Teachers can also post their lessons and resources on the network so that students and parents can access them from any Internet connection. Once lessons are in a digital format, they can be easily adjusted or updated by teachers for future use.

Although traditional computer labs cannot provide continuous access for all students, they can enhance learning opportunities by providing access to online information, assessments, and daily classes scheduled by teachers. Computer labs are also being used effectively to provide advanced placement opportunities and other online courses.

Cell phones remain controversial in the educational setting. Very few schools are supplying smartphones to students. Schools often require students to shut off their phones during the school day and punish those who are seen using them. However, this technology is being used in several instructionally appropriate ways. For example, cell phones are being adapted for use as response clickers, students are using the stopwatch function in science labs and physical education, and students are using the camera function to take pictures for media presentations.

Because one of the core strengths of technology is its ability to personalize instruction, it is interesting to note the frequency with which intervention classes use technology. At least 80% of respondents report weekly use of technology for Title I, reading intervention, and special education. Clearly, a well-qualified teacher remains the single most important component in reading intervention, but technology can help students quickly make progress in areas of decoding, in which they are deficient.

Technology is used less frequently for English language learners (ELL) but still at least weekly in 72% of respondent schools. The frequent use of technology in social studies (at least weekly in 79% of respondent schools) and science indicates the important attributes of digital content—currency, accessibility, and modularity. Original documents, often available online through search engines, lend authenticity and reality, while viewing opposing positions on current events online supports lively discussion and debate.

Finally, the lower usage of technology in world languages indicates that offsetting cost savings in this subject area may be possible because these classes might be using expensive single-purpose language labs. In the case of 4-to-1 and higher-ratio schools, the lower usage levels in science, ELL, social studies, and career tech indicate that the students in this environment are not enjoying the benefits of technology.

Ubiquitous technology programs face difficult financial and philosophical challenges in today's economic climate, in which superintendents and school boards must often cut programs and lay off teachers. In an era of high-stakes test scores and teacher accountability, it can be difficult to motivate teachers and administrators to move to more student-centered learning. And because the benefits of a ubiquitous educational technology program are realized over several years, many schools opt for short-term fixes and stopgap measures.

Critical thinking and information literacy based on real-world activities are skills that students have needed for generations. However, the need is greater than ever today because learning offers a strategic advantage in our competitive global environment. Educators have generally underestimated the challenge of teaching these skills in the context of real-world content, but in technology-rich schools, they are making a realistic assessment of the needs and moving ahead with major changes in curriculum, teaching, and learning.

Technology Implications for Cost Savings

Personalized instruction that meets each student's needs offers a greater chance for on-time or early college matriculation, thus reducing the cost of remedial coursework at the college level. In addition, learners with 21st-century skills will be competitively positioned in the global marketplace and more likely to achieve success, leading to a skilled workforce and an increased tax base.

Under the Obama administration, technology funding is now part of regular instructional programs rather than a separate funding stream such as Enhancing Education Through Technology (EETT). In subjects such as math, where technology can help bridge the gap between the U.S. and other countries, funding is available from more sources than ever before. School finance officials should check with the Association of School Business Officials (ASBO) and the National Council of Teachers of Mathematics (NCTM) for current information about funding streams from both public and private sources.

As mobile computing devices continue to replace desktops, the potential for cost savings will increase, for example, by replacing textbooks with digital content. However, this cost benefit can only be realized when all students have continuous access to a computing device connected to the Internet. Paper and copying costs will also decline, and efficiencies in testing, grading, and reporting will increase.

Stable and robust networks are costly. However, the opportunity cost of idle equipment and an underutilized network is even greater. It is important that school leaders understand the financial and physical network requirements to handle the amount and types of usage needed.

Most schools will find it relatively easy to connect all teachers at home as well as at school. Leading-edge schools should be able to provide 3G–4G coverage for teachers at a cost of approximately $25 per teacher per month.

While most schools have networks, an estimated 90% of schools will need to update their networks in the future to accommodate increased usage. The most common upgrades and their financial impact are as follows:

Wireless networks. Currently networks are predominantly 802.11b or 802.11g, and the wireless networks are not designed for 1-to-1 use. State-of-the-art networks are 802.11n and designed to support multiple megabits/second/student. They also offer more advanced quality of service (QOS) and security than today's wireless networks.

- **Estimated financial impact.** $80 per student, one-time capital equipment investment.

Internet connections/bandwidth. The current Internet capacity is roughly 10 kilobits/second/student. In a future 1-to-1 environment, this will need to grow tenfold.

- **Estimated financial impact.** $20 per student per year, ongoing expense.

Support of student-owned devices. Today, most schools ban student-owned devices as security risks. In the future, schools will need to support student-owned devices extensively. This will require upgrades to hardware and software in many cases.

- **Estimated financial impact.** $10 per student hardware, $3 per student in annual software fees.

24/7 3G–4G student connectivity. Today this is very rare. As 4G deployments increase, the cost per megabit drops. As of this writing, the FCC has announced a competitive pilot program for student 3G–4G wireless support. Ubiquitous connectivity is an integral part of the high-performance school of the future.

- **Estimated financial impact.** $20 to $75 per student per year, depending on the amount of bandwidth per student. This assumes E-Rate support or new carrier pricing models.

Connectivity for financially disadvantaged students. Every district has students whose households cannot afford home Internet access. To support the learning platforms of the future, every student will need to be connected at home. The range of need is from 1% to 30% of students.

- **Estimated financial impact.** $15 per student per month for those in need.

Appropriate bandwidth available throughout the school community can be expensive and complicated. Bandwidth issues may reside in locations that the school does not control, and the district may have to pay for bandwidth both inside and outside of the district. It is essential that districts understand the entire bandwidth pipeline and the expenses associated with providing bandwidth to meet the needs of the implementation.

Secure access for parents can help build communication between home and school. However, schools must recognize the challenges some parents face in accessing the network. Schools may need to budget for parent training or computer lab access for parents at school. Until all parents have reasonably simple access to the instructional network, it will be impossible to abandon the traditional, less efficient, and more expensive forms of communication.

Technology Implications for Policy

Our survey shows that well-implemented technology programs have enabled personalized instruction and the development of 21st-century skills, pointing to the need for policies that foster uninterrupted access to technology and related professional learning. The policies that need to be re-examined include those that require Carnegie units (seat time) for course credit and those that require a teacher to be present at all times (a requirement that is often inappropriate for blended online and offline learning).

Strong Title I funding is needed for the purchase of software in technology-augmented intervention classes. These curriculum purchases for daily use are more likely to be in urban areas with higher minority percentages and lower household incomes than the average. Intervention programs for struggling students have used technology more frequently than traditional subject areas—possibly the result of the higher funding per student for remediation. The strong desire of U.S. schools to improve science, technology, engineering, and mathematics (STEM) learning may drive the next wave of integrated use of technology for collaborative learning. To increase our nation's competitiveness, policymakers should make more funding available for intervention and STEM subjects, including technology-augmented programs.

The Project RED data do suggest that connectivity is correlated with affluence and that students in poor schools are more likely to have slower connections.

School districts should integrate teacher use of technology into their overall assessment of teachers, to speed up the adoption of technology as an integral part of the learning process by those teachers who might be reluctant to change. It is clear from our respondents that technology use is not expected or mandated in many environments. Key policy decisions should also include when and how to connect all teachers and whether or not to provide 3G–4G wireless connectivity off campus. Most districts and states will need to overhaul their connectivity plans in light of the many upcoming changes. Key policy decisions will also include when and how to support student-owned devices, including cell phones, and provide wireless Internet access off school premises (3G–4G); what level of support to provide to the economically disadvantaged; and what new funding sources might be required, including new taxes to support a state-level E-Rate–like program.

A lack of appropriate network infrastructure inhibits the usefulness of the devices. Policymakers might want to require that local education authorities provide appropriate infrastructure and support plans for devices purchased with public funding.

Schools are moving to mobile computing at a breakneck pace, affecting many aspects of the school environment. Policymakers must address the issues of safety, privacy, and cyberbullying before individual schools become too restrictive, as well as addressing the realities of the digital divide. The digital divide exists not only between one student group and another but also between students and parents. As devices and networks become more widespread, free public access to computing devices and the Internet will become increasingly important to ensure that students and parents are connected and some groups are not left out. Despite extensive national discussions about the lack of bandwidth in the U.S., the Project RED survey seems to indicate that bandwidth is not an issue for most schools. This is misleading, as 68% of schools are already extensively limiting high bandwidth applications. However, it would be prudent to closely examine the bandwidth issue at the state and national levels and to work toward completing a national wired and wireless grid to expand usage.

Technology Implications for Industry

The move to mobile computing affects all segments of the educational technology industry. It is important to be aware that computers in schools are aging at an alarming rate, and funding for replacements is dwindling just as fast. Unfortunately, schools are not thinking in terms of refresh cycles in the current environment of strong budget constraints.

The new paradigm of student-centered learning and individualized instruction creates a need for new materials and classroom designs. Although the concept of authentic learning has been discussed for some time, it remains a major growth area for developers of high-quality real-world math and science content, and providers of teacher training that focuses on authentic learning.

Although hardware manufacturers are well aware of the shift from desktop to mobile computing, too little research and development is going into this segment. Most devices were developed for the consumer or business markets and are not optimized for schools. Because school volumes are not huge, the argument can be made that there is no need for a custom product, but schools might argue that they would buy more if a product truly met their needs.

It is essential that the instructional platform within the network is secure and easy to navigate. Teachers must be able to easily post to the network lessons and assignment guidelines for students. Students must be able to easily work through lessons, post completed assignments back to the network for teacher review, and efficiently communicate with teachers throughout the process. There will be a major sales opportunity based on the forecast improvements in connectivity. In several areas, including support of 3G–4G to students, some invention will be required to reach desired price and functionality targets. As in the case of the system reliability implications, it would be helpful if vendors could provide bandwidth specifications per active user, for each software package, that would take into account individual district requirements, such as the number of devices and the levels and types of usage the local education agency (LEA) is planning.

Parents also need a platform within the instructional network that is secure and easy to navigate. If these conditions are not met, it is highly unlikely that parents will access the network on a daily, or even on a frequent, basis. Because there may be limited opportunities for training, parents must be able to easily find and understand their child's records and other information pertinent to their child's education.

Conclusion

Personalized instruction is one of the strongest benefits of technology and one of the most critical factors in 21st-century education. To help students achieve, it is essential to address their unique learning needs, generally in small-group and one-on-one situations, and to move from a teacher-centered to a learner-centered environment. Schools with good technology implementations follow these practices. They also provide students with consistent access to digital resources, ensuring a dynamic rather than a static educational setting.

CHAPTER 7

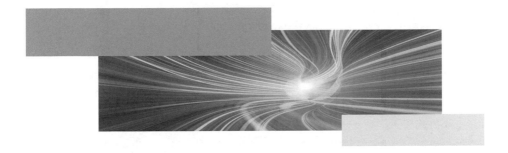

Technology Implementation: Impetus, Funding, Assessment, Sustainability

When the research was completed, mobile devices constituted 45% of the computing devices used in schools (laptops, netbooks, tablets, and smartphones). The move to mobile computing is likely to support the transition from teacher-centered to student-centered learning. In both environments the teacher is essential, but in the latter, the teacher has more time for one-on-one student interaction. Mobile computing also provides freedom of location. Students can work in small groups, individually, or in large groups, inside or outside of the classroom. The potential for personalized learning also increases in a digital learning environment. To be effective learning tools, digital materials need to be portable and available wherever a book would be available—which is only possible with mobile devices.

Because schools are built to last 40 years or more, school design and the need for in-classroom desktop computers must be revisited in light of the transition to mobile ubiquitous computing. Continuous personal access to a mobile computing device and the Internet dramatically expands the intellectual resources available to students and ensures a dynamic, rather than static, education setting.

The Impetus for Technology Initiatives

School districts increasingly view technology as supporting the teaching and learning mission, rather than as a goal in itself. One-third of survey respondents cite the enhancement of student learning as the rationale for their technology initiative. The second highest response (21% of respondents) report that the original impetus was to help students build the skills they need in order to participate in the 21st-century workforce.

Note that regardless of a school's student–computer ratio, the primary drivers of a technology initiative are enhancing student learning and preparing students for today's workforce. That is, the primary drivers of a technology initiative are not issues such as "closing the digital divide," availability of funding, adequate yearly progress (AYP) concerns, the academic standing of a particular school, or top-down mandates. The percentage of respondents that cited any of these issues was very low, under 5%. The exception was funding, which was cited by 9% of 4-to-1 or higher schools and 7% of 3-to-1 or 2-to-1 schools.

Because instructional technology is no longer a line item in federal grants, school finance officers should look to business operations and infrastructure as a place to fund productivity investments. Technology advocates in schools should continue to focus on funding instructional solutions that meet the needs of high-risk, special education, and English language learners.

The lack of a clear education goal is one of the main reasons technology initiatives fail. Creators of grants and special initiatives should build in clear objectives and measurements throughout the life of the grant. Many grant applications lack a clear objective and, even more frequently, a clear process for assessing progress toward the goal after the grant is awarded.

Funding Sources for Technology Initiatives

The funding for technology initiatives in America's schools comes from numerous sources. The Project RED data reveals that for most (72%) respondents, one funding source for their technology initiatives was their operating budget or capital budget. Almost half (42%) of respondents report using formula grants from state or federal sources, reflecting the frequent use of Title I (NCLB) funding for technology purchases as well as various innovative program-funding sources. Many also point to E-Rate funding. Surprisingly, only 17% of respondents cite Enhancing Education Through Technology (EETT) funds as a source for funding their technology initiative. It is worth noting that, on average, 2.1 funding sources were identified per respondent. The accompanying table shows the funding sources for a technology initiative, in terms of the percentage of Project RED respondents reporting.

Funding Sources for Technology Initiative

Funding Source	Percentage of Respondents (%)*
Operating budget or capital budget	72
Formula grants from state or federal sources	42
Competitive grants (other than EETT)	22
Bond issue (or similar)	17
Enhancing Education Through Technology (EETT)	17
Foundation for private individual	15
Other	13
Shift to funding from textbooks to technology	9
Special taxes	4
* Multiple answers allowed.	

Source: Project RED (www.projectred.org)

Funding technology from the regular operating budget allows technology to be integrated into the curricular budget, paralleling the integration of technology into the curriculum. This follows the federal government lead in reducing the dependence on technology-specific funding sources, such as EETT. Many respondents note that they started with a grant but continued to fund through operating expenses. Others were unable to continue funding technology when grant money ceased.

School operating budgets often provide stable financing for ongoing purchases and support, a major shift from the 1990s when bond issues provided most funding. However, given the current state of school budgets, schools may cut back on technology programs and tech support staff if they are part of the regular operating budget.

Policymakers can consider some new alternatives to the funding conundrum. Education leaders can consider adapting their systems to accept the technologies that students already own, such as cell phones and laptop computers. Some districts are moving in this direction. For example, Plano Independent School District in Texas is leveraging student-owned devices by providing robust wireless access at all sites. Students can connect devices they bring.

A more stable funding base has both advantages and disadvantages. Major project initiatives will still require substantial funding sources, but day-to-day purchases and support will benefit from funding through the regular budget. While bond issues and special taxes are cited by less than 25% of respondents, they may still be the fuel for major initiatives and upgrades.

Parents are a primary influencer of bond issues and other funding measures, meaning that schools need to develop parents as both information sources and spokespersons. An outreach public relations program that uses materials from the Association of School Business Officials International (ASBO), the National School Boards Association (NSBA), and other organizations can provide valuable content for busy school officials.

Numerous surveys, such as National Association of Colleges and Employers 2007, have indicated that parents have high education aspirations for their children. Policymakers should view technology as one way to advance this agenda. The Project RED finding that parents in less affluent areas are more likely to have less involvement suggests a strong need for programs that engage parents, and perhaps enable parental access to instructional networks.

Assessing the Effectiveness of a Technology Initiative

The single most important factor for success in a technology implementation is leadership. Implementations driven by the vision and goals of leaders are much more likely to be successful than implementations driven by the sudden availability of funds. Therefore, school-level leadership must assess its own work in order to properly determine the effectiveness of a technology initiative.

Three quarters of respondents report that teacher training, teacher buy-in, service and support, and the instructional network were addressed well or adequately in the technology implementation plan. More than half (55%) of respondents report that long-term funding was addressed very well or adequately. Only 33% report that parent involvement was addressed very well or adequately.

Across all measures, 1-to-1 schools outperform schools with higher student–computer ratios. Notably, about three quarters (76%) of schools with 1-to-1 programs report adequate planning for long-term funding, far more than other schools. Effectiveness of teacher training is reported to be more adequate in 1-to-1 schools than in schools with higher student–computer ratios. The biggest reported difference between 1-to-1 schools and other schools is in parent training. Almost twice as many 1-to-1 schools report successful parent training when compared to schools with higher student–computer ratios. The school finance environment tends to focus on the short term, with single-year rather than five-year plans. However, creative long-term financing, such as the leasing of equipment, can help smooth out costs and allow for more timely maintenance and continuity of instruction.

Parental involvement must be included as part of any technology initiative. It appears that some grants, such as Title I grants, are already doing this, as evidenced by the high percentage of schools with high poverty percentages reporting that parent training was handled well, in contrast to schools with lower poverty (schools with high poverty percentages are far more likely than schools with lower poverty percentages to receive Title I and E-Rate federal funding). However, three-quarters of respondents gave C-to-failing grades to all phases of the technology implementation concerning parent training.

Clearly the days of "we got the funding, let's go" must be replaced with cabinet-level and system-wide planning. The Project RED Roadmap Checklist in Appendix B can function as an integral part of the project management plan so that no district has to start from scratch.

Sustainability of a Technology Initiative

The belief that a technology program is sustainable for two, three, or five years allows the program to become embedded in curriculum. When a technology program is viewed as a test, long-term plans cannot be made. Project RED data reveal that 6% of respondents feel their program is sustainable for one year or less. More than half (56%) of respondents feel their program is sustainable for five years or more. It is worth noting that 38 respondents did not answer this question in the Project RED survey, suggesting a lack of knowledge or communication on this aspect of a technology initiative. The accompanying table shows the sustainability of a technology initiative, as reported by respondents to Project RED.

Sustainability of a Technology Initiative

Duration	Percentage of Respondents (%)
One year or less	6
Two years	12
Three years or more	26
Five years or more	56

Source: Project RED (www.projectred.org)

One of the early problems with technology purchases in schools was the lack of long-term funding, driven by the nature of school finance. Rather than commit to a single major investment in technology, education leaders can explore leasing programs and other creative financing options that can spread technology costs over time.

Since World War II, school budgets have grown at twice the rate of inflation, yet long-term planning is still not a consistent practice. Education is one of the most service-intensive industries in the country, yet it lags far behind in using technology to reduce costs and improve processes. Indeed, school district budgets are often set up to "hide" or "save" cost reductions with little or no reward for economic measures. States and other stakeholders should examine the negative financial implications of many state practices and work toward improvement in processes and cost reductions as part of its mandates, with part of the savings going back to the schools and districts.

CHAPTER 8

Positive Outcomes

In this chapter we focus on the positive outcomes often seen following successful educational technology implementations. We look first at all grades generally and then focus on high school, providing recommendations in four areas: instruction, cost savings, policy, and industry. For a deep dive into the data that led us to these recommendations, please refer to our full report, *The Technology Factor: Nine Keys to Student Achievement and Cost-Effectiveness* (Greaves et al., 2010; available at www.projectred.org).

Impact of Technology: All Grades

Technology changes schools. The financial measures for a technology implementation in schools can include costs associated with paperwork, test scores, school attendance rates, course completion and graduation rates for students.

The majority (80%) of Project RED respondents report that paperwork has been greatly or somewhat reduced because of implementation of technology. Most (67%) respondents report that paper and copy machine expenses have been greatly or somewhat reduced. More than half (53%) of respondents report that the number of disciplinary actions has been greatly or somewhat reduced. The majority (69%) of respondents report that high-stakes test scores have greatly or somewhat improved. Nearly half (48%) of respondents report that dropout rates have greatly or somewhat improved; and one quarter (25%) of respondents report that teacher attendance has greatly or somewhat improved.

Note that test scores do not appear to be improving at a greater rate in average 1-to-1 schools than in schools with higher ratios. Proper implementation appears to be more important than the student–computer ratio for improving test scores. A school with a 4-to-1 ratio that enjoys good leadership, teacher collaboration, and frequent online communication in a mentoring environment may have better outcomes than a 1-to-1 school that implements none of the Project RED Key Implementation Factors (see Chapter 3).

Instruction

Administrators, teachers, staff, and others benefit from time savings because of paperwork reduction. The actual savings depend on many factors but in a NextSchool, for example (see Chapter 10), the savings estimate is about a 2% reduction in the teacher's time. When aggregated, this can translate to large time savings.

Moreover, reducing paperwork across-the-board improves productivity and frees up time for teachers and administrators to focus on improving job performance and enhancing instruction. As a result, drop-out rates decrease, which reduces costs associated with remediation if the student returns to school. Moreover, students are better prepared for the realities of the post-secondary education and workforce demands of the 21st century.

Cost Savings

A reduction in paper and copy machine expenses can free up funds for student-focused areas or ameliorate cost increases and revenue reductions. Teachers report that a reduction in paperwork can lead to five extra instructional minutes per class period, which translates to an increase of 15 potential instructional days per year.

In terms of the financial impact on society as a whole, studies show that students who attend college or who are jointly enrolled in high school and college enjoy significantly higher annual earnings, leading to increased tax revenue that benefits the economy and legislative priorities, such as education.

Policy

School and district policies must be in place to fully realize the savings and increased productivity that result from reduced paperwork, for example, through workflow re-engineering that adjusts roles and responsibilities. The expectation that schools will acquire technology and use it well must be embedded in policy. When technology is well integrated, policymakers can begin shifting some of the resources allocated for staffing and legacy expenses to contemporary processes that provide greater return on investment.

District, state, and national policies can further require that data be used to drive decisions regarding staffing, course offerings, student education plans, and more, so that districts and schools make expenditures that have been shown to make a difference in schools.

Industry

As schools transform to digital environments, robust technology tools for classroom, clerical, and administrative purposes will be increasingly in demand. A whole system approach will be the order of the day, with just-in-time data retrieval that drives best practices and one point of registration from which information is accessible as students move through the grades.

Looking beyond the educational technology industry, the implications for the service, construction, and manufacturing sectors are substantial because working-age adults who are better educated exhibit improved time on task skills, attendance, critical thinking and problem solving skills, personal growth, and organizational and individual earnings potential.

Impact of Technology: High Schools

The implementation of technology affects the efficiency of instructional delivery and prepares students for college. It positively affects student outcomes in course completion, graduation rates, and college attendance. These three factors, in turn, come together to lay the bedrock for effective, efficient, and cost-conscious school programming.

In practical terms, these factors can be best understood in terms of student dual or joint college enrollment, college attendance plans, advanced placement (AP) course enrollment, course completion rates, and graduation rates. Well over half (66%) of respondents report that dual or joint enrollment in college has greatly or somewhat increased. More than half (58%) of respondents report that the number of students who have established college attendance plans has greatly or somewhat increased. About half (47%) of respondents report that AP course enrollment has greatly or somewhat increased. More than half (59%) of respondents report that course completion rates have greatly or somewhat increased. About half (54%) of respondents report that graduation rates have greatly or somewhat increased.

Across all measures detailed here, leaders of schools with a 1-to-1 student–computer ratio report improvements in student outcomes that are superior to those from leaders of schools with higher student–computer ratios.

Instruction

Increased dual enrollment in high school and college courses provides more personalized education and expedites pathways to matriculation. Increased course completion rates mean that fewer students drop out and need remediation after high school; and when students develop a roadmap of the courses and skills they need to reach their academic and career goals, they make more plans for higher education.

Dual and joint enrollment allows students to personalize and pursue instructional goals generally available only in the postsecondary environment, thus reducing college costs for families and states. Moreover, when students attain some college objectives while still in high school, student engagement in the workforce is expedited and contributions to state revenue increase.

Finally, increased AP course enrollment allows the learning experience to be individualized, which means that students can achieve at the highest levels, reduce the number of courses taken at the post-high school level, and matriculate earlier in college.

Cost Savings

For districts and institutions of higher education, an increase in AP course enrollment—combined with increased high-stakes test scores, increased graduation rates, and decreased discipline referrals—can result in less student remediation and thus reduced expenses. When more students are enrolled in AP courses and more students complete college courses in high school, post-secondary costs are reduced, moderating overall tax burdens.

When teacher attendance improves, substitute teacher costs are reduced, including the operational costs associated with finding and hiring substitutes. When high-stakes test scores improve, remediation time is reduced, and student outcomes improve within a constant metric of dollars and time invested. When the need for disciplinary action is reduced, administrators and teachers expend less time on behavior issues and more time on student learning, while remaining within existing budgets.

There is also a financial impact on society as a whole. When high school students pursue AP and dual enrollment opportunities, families benefit from reduced higher education tuition expense. When graduation rates increase, annual and lifetime income also increases, which increases overall tax revenues.

Policy

Policymakers must provide incentives that encourage schools to adopt cost-saving measures along with mechanisms to capture the savings, rather than having them disappear into the system.

National, state, and district policies can require that schools provide access to AP and dual enrollment opportunities, as well as the preliminary scaffolding through a standards-based curriculum. Technology tools provide efficient ways to reach these goals. With efficient technology integration throughout the instructional program, systems will become more effective and student achievement will flourish.

Industry

Schools and districts need resources that support individualized learning and tools that provide immediate personal feedback to students and teachers. Data systems that allow for just-in-time student progress data will give districts and schools the ability to make decisions and plan based on pre- and post-high school coursework.

Conclusion

The implementation of technology has broad-based positive impacts on schools across grade levels. As we have seen, the positive outcomes from such an initiative can be considered in terms of financial savings, academic achievement for students, and improved efficiencies for the educational system as a whole. In the next chapter, we will continue the cost savings discussion with a deeper dive into the subject.

CHAPTER 9

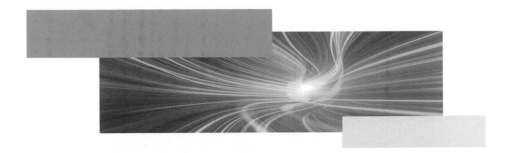

Cost Reduction Deep Dive

This chapter closely examines the many categories of savings provided by properly implemented educational technology, providing a better understanding of the cost-benefit picture of technology-transformed learning.

Implementation Costs

The cost of technology implementations can vary widely. For example, the reported cost for 1-to-1 implementations range from $250 per student per year to more than $1,000 per student per year, measured on a four-year refresh cycle. There are many cost drivers. The following are a few of the key variables:

- **Type of hardware.** The cost difference between a netbook or handheld device versus full-featured laptop can be significant.

- **Refresh cycles.** These range from three years to six years or longer.

- **Professional development.** Districts report a range of $1 to $100 per student per year.

- **Amount of software.** Annualized software costs range from $25 per student per year to more than $100 per student per year.

The following section details two cost scenarios. We tried to be conservative in our estimates. Many school districts have found ways to cut costs while maintaining program quality. An example is a district that self-insures and uses student technicians to do first-level tech support and repair laptops as a for-credit course.

Examples of Implementation Costs

This first example examines a school with one computer for every three students, made up of a combination of classroom and lab computers. The second example examines a 1-to-1 school able to fully exploit second-order change and provide extensive professional development and support. Both examples are presumed to be new schools, because in existing schools there would be a wide range of pre-existing hardware, software, and infrastructure. In both schools, the Project RED analysis assumes the following:

- 500 students, 25 teachers and staff

- 20 classrooms

- 10 common areas (library, cafeteria, and so forth)

- Student and teacher hardware with a useful life of four years

- Infrastructure costs for wireless LANs, etc., amortized over seven years

- Hardware costs amortized over four years and full warranty with protection for accidental damage; there is a 5% loaner pool for the 1-to-1 laptop program

- Not included: Space savings and power savings
- Not included: Consumable costs, such as paper and toner

A simplified set of implementation costs for these two examples are expressed in the accompanying table. (For an expanded version of this table, please contact the Project RED team at info@projectred.org.)

Implementation Costs: Traditional versus Technology-Transformed Schools

Example 1: Traditional School 3-to-1 Student–Computer Ratio		Example 2: Technology-Transformed School 1-to-1 Student–Computer Ratio	
Hardware			
$101	Cost per student per year	$255	Cost per student per year
Servers, router, firewall, and related software			
$13	Cost per student per year	$25	Cost per student per year
Annualized software costs			
$96	Cost per student per year	$128	Cost per student per year
Wireless network			
$14	Cost per student per year	$22	Cost per student per year
Telecom			
$5	Cost per student per year @ 10 Kb/sec/ student average	$25	Cost per student per year @ 50 Kb/sec/ student average
Tech support			
$38	Cost per student per year	$75	Cost per student per year
Professional development			
$31	Cost per student per year	$63	Cost per student per year
Total Costs			
$298	Total cost per student per year	$593	Total cost per student per year

Source: Project RED (www.projectred.org)

The cost differential between these two schools is roughly $295 per student per year. It is worth noting that these costs will decline over time. Because it would take a state at least seven years to fully implement 1-to-1 computing from initial planning to last student device purchased, the 1-to-1 implementation cost at the end of that period could be the same as a 3-to-1 implementation today.

More importantly, the technology-transformed solution enables second-order changes and financial advantages that far outweigh the cost differential.

Impact on ESMs and Financial Variables

A technology-transformed environment affects numerous Education Success Measures (ESMs) and financial variables, which the Project RED team examined with regard to three types of impact:

- **Cost avoidance.** These savings result when a current practice ceases; for example, when free online primary source materials replace purchased materials.

- **Cost savings.** These savings result when technology provides a less expensive way to perform a function; for example, when parent newsletters are sent out electronically rather than on paper.

- **Revenue enhancements.** These savings are the additional tax revenues that result when students are better trained and enjoy higher incomes.

It should be noted that this chapter does not discuss the variables that could result from truly significant second-order re-engineering. Moreover, the impact of each item is highly dependent on local issues. For example, some schools have a huge number of dropouts, while others do not.

Dropout and Graduation Rates

Dropouts undoubtedly have the highest financial impact of any of the variables discussed in this book. The primary reason is that students who avoid dropping out and who go on to college have substantially increased earning power and consequently pay more taxes. These increased tax payments continue throughout the careers of these individuals.

Nationally, 25% of all students drop out, or roughly a million students a year. Project RED estimates that the average dropout-student fails at least six classes before dropping out. Given an average cost per class of $1,333, the direct avoidable cost is approximately $8,000. The human cost, however, is incalculable and can span generations.

The number of Project RED schools reporting a reduction in dropouts because of improved technology jumps to 89% when the Project RED Key Implementation Factors are employed. A student who graduates from high school could generate $166,000 to $353,000 in increased tax revenues compared with a dropout. A dropout who would have gone on to college could have generated an additional $448,000 to $874,000 in tax revenue over a career of 40 years.

- **National-level savings.** $3 trillion per year after 40 years of a higher taxpaying workforce, or $56,273 per student per year.

Post-Secondary Remedial Education

Despite meeting graduation requirements, roughly a third of today's high school graduates require some level of remedial education in basic skills, a percentage that climbs as the job or course rigor increases. For example, 75% of freshmen entering the University of California system require at least one remedial course—and these are students who represent the cream of their high school graduating class.

Remediation places a financial burden on employers and post-secondary institutions. These remediation costs can be understood in the following ways:

- The cost of reteaching basic skills at the college or university level.

- The increased expenses of reteaching, which results in lower tax revenues.

- The longer time needed to receive a post-secondary degree, which results in loss of income and tax revenues.

- The likelihood that students who require remediation will not complete college, which results in long-term loss of tax revenue.

The total annual cost at a national level is estimated at $16.6 billion a year.

- **National-level savings.** $1.6 billion a year or $30 per student per year, based on only a 10% reduction in remediation costs because of better-performing high schools.

Teacher Attendance

Project RED found that teacher attendance improves in 1-to-1 school environments. These teacher attendance costs can be understood in the following ways:

- The cost of substitute teachers.

- The cost of finding, qualifying, and scheduling substitute teachers.

- The impact on learning when taught by substitutes versus regular teachers.

The number of Project RED schools reporting teacher attendance increases goes up 20% when the top four Project RED Key Implementation Factors are employed.

- **National-level savings.** $715 million a year, based on a 1% increase in teacher attendance, leading to savings of $13 per student per year.

Copy Machine Costs

Copy machine costs are an easy-to-understand proxy for the savings potential of re-engineering. Copy machine costs can be understood in the following ways:

- $100,000 in paper and copy machine costs for a 1,500 student high school.

- 2 million copies a year or 1,333 copies per student per year, or 7.4 copies per student per day at 4 cents per copy for the paper and the machine use.

- An estimated labor cost of one penny per page, assuming the machine makes copies at 30 pages a minute, and another penny per page for distribution.

In Project RED-surveyed schools where students use a learning management system (LMS) many times a day, 20% more schools report reductions in copy machine expenses. If the LMS is used only daily (versus many times a day), the number of schools reporting copy cost reductions drops from 20% to 6%. Note that once-a-day LMS use indicates casual use to check calendars, and so on. Multiple times a day use indicates more integral use of a LMS, such as to upload and download assignments, take online courses, and collaborate with others.

- **National-level savings.** $2.2 billion a year, based on annual savings of $40 per student per year, a 50% reduction in expenses.

Online Formative Assessments

Online formative assessments have financial advantages, but more importantly, they provide valuable real-time feedback to both teachers and students regarding student performance levels.

Test printing costs 3 to 4 cents per page. Tests run from 1 to 10 pages, and students often take one test a month in each of five classes, or 50 tests a year. At nine pages a test and 3 cents a page, the cost is $13.50 per student per year. Manual scoring takes one to three minutes per multiple-choice test. If teacher time is worth 30 cents to 60 cents per minute, the cost is roughly 30 cents to $2 per test, including recording in the grade book, returning tests, and so forth. Assuming 50 tests a year and 50 cents a test, the cost is $25 per student per year.

Online assessment uses a computing system to create, store, deliver, and score test items—on a local computer, a networked computer, or via cloud computing. These functions are frequently performed by a LMS or a more specialized testing system. Teachers can select high-quality test items based on a specific state standard and create a test. As the industry matures, standards such as QTI (IMS Question and Test Interoperability) are contributing to features such as the ability to reuse items and combine item banks from multiple suppliers.

The benefits and savings of online formative assessments can be understood in the following ways:

- Reduced paper and printing costs for exam booklets.

- Reduced teacher time spent on scoring. If scanner scoring is used, the cost can be cut in half to $12.50 per student per year.

- Second-order changes:

    - Shorter test times

    - More time for instruction

    - Easier tailoring to class circumstances

    - More frequent tests for ongoing feedback

    - More teachable moments based on immediate feedback

    - Automatic essay grading

- **National-level savings.** More than $2.4 billion a year, based on $44 per student per year.

High-Stakes Test Scores and College Attendance Plans

Increases in high-stakes test scores imply that fewer students are failing. They also correlate to improved college attendance, increased long-term tax revenues, and reduced test-prep expenses.

Advanced high school students can take advanced placement (AP) courses or college-level courses via dual or joint enrollment, allowing them to graduate from college earlier. Students and their families save money on college expenses. States benefit by reduced subsidies to state institutions and by receiving income tax revenues earlier. Although AP courses generally cost more per student than ordinary high school courses, AP courses provide significant cost benefits similar to the benefits of dual/joint enrollment.

Project RED conservatively estimates that states provide up to $1,000 per course in subsidies to colleges and universities. It is worth noting that according to the U.S. Department of Education's National Center for Education Statistics, in 2008 the total subsidy was $9,677 per student. Assuming five courses, this is $1,935 per student per course.

If 50% of high school graduates go to state-funded colleges and each of these students takes one college-level course, the net savings to the states is $500 per student or $1 billion a year at the national level.

On a household scale, each college course taken in high school saves a student and family approximately $2,000. Moreover, students who take dual/joint enrollment or AP courses often graduate earlier and get jobs earlier. Their income increases at graduation, along with the sales taxes, property taxes, and income taxes they pay.

- **National-level savings.** If students in technology-transformed high schools where educational technology has been properly implemented take two or more college-level courses, the net savings to the states is $3.2 billion or $58 per student per year.

Paperwork Reduction

Teachers and other school personnel have a significant paperwork burden. Teacher time saved on paperwork can be spent with students. The total cost of paperwork is tangible but difficult to quantify. Many teachers report dissatisfaction with the burden of paperwork and the loss of teaching time.

Teacher time saved from reduced paperwork can be reallocated to additional student-facing time. Additional student-facing time should yield improvements in areas such as dropouts, disciplinary actions, joint enrollment, and high-stakes test scores. Assuming a paperwork reduction yields a 5% improvement in the above areas, an incremental $50 per student can be saved. Note that 100% of the Project RED schools that deploy the top four Project RED Key Implementation Factors report a paperwork reduction because of technology.

A technology-transformed school produces additional teacher capacity, and that capacity can be made available for an increase in class size. For example, if two minutes, or 4% of time, are saved per class period, one additional student can be supported. If, for example, the yearly expenditure per student in average daily attendance (ADA) is $8,000, and assuming 50% of this amount is allocated to teachers' salaries, then $129 per student can be saved, amortized over the class. These savings could go toward increasing teachers' salaries or other worthwhile uses.

Finally, in a technology-transformed school, the savings to administrators, staff, and others could be 2%, which could lead to a head count reduction. This reduction could be converted to a per-student savings.

- **National-level savings.** From $3.3 billion to $7.1 billion per year, based on an average savings of $60 to $129 per student per year, assuming the savings can be recaptured.

Disciplinary Actions

Disciplinary actions cost schools money. These actions also consume a substantial amount of time for administrators, teachers, and clerical staff.

Disciplinary actions reduce instructional time and affect outcomes for all students. Serious issues require police intervention. The cost to the taxpayer of a police visit is $100 or more. Some schools need full-time police presence or contracted security guards at a cost of approximately $50 per student per year.

Suspensions frequently result in legal fees. One school district reported $250,000 in legal fees for a case that went to trial.

Schools with low rates of disciplinary actions can reasonably expect a 10% cost reduction by adhering to the Project RED Key Implementation Factors. Schools with challenging disciplinary action rates can experience a reduction of 50% or more.

Leaders from the majority (92%) of Project RED 1-to-1 schools that deploy the top four Key Implementation Factors report a reduction in disciplinary action, which is an improvement of 37 points over all 1-to-1 schools. For example, Mooresville Graded School District in North Carolina (5,409 students) reported that short-term suspensions and expulsions dropped from 549 to 310, and long-term suspensions and expulsions dropped from 7 to 4 after the district moved to a properly implemented 1-to-1 solution.

- **National-level savings.** $1.1 billion a year for middle and high schools, based on an average savings of $20 per student per year.

End-of-Course Failure

When a student fails a course, there is a significant cost to reteach the course. Course failure is also a leading indicator of future dropouts. Retained students increase the school population, contributing to teaching costs, overcrowding, and additional costs (such as portable buildings). The cost to the district and state of reteaching the course is $1,333, or higher in the case of intervention-type courses. End-of-course failure can be devastating to students and increase the likelihood they will drop out.

About one quarter (26%) of schools report a reduction in end-of-course failure when they apply the Project RED Key Implementation Factors.

- **National-level savings.** $5.9 billion a year if technology-transformed schools where educational technology has been properly implemented experience a 20% reduction in end-of-course failure. Currently 40% of students fail classes such as algebra; but with properly implemented technology the net result would be 8% fewer failures, or a savings of $107 per student per year or $5.9 billion on a national level.

Digital versus Print Supplemental Materials

Digital content can be repurposed, accessed anytime and anywhere, searched according to a number of criteria, chunked and reused, tagged and stored in a content management system (CMS) or a learning management system (LMS) with CMS features. This content can be classified and indexed in a variety of ways, easily uploaded, stored on flash drives, and re-used on demand.

Schools spend more than $3.4 billion a year on supplemental print materials. Some of these materials cannot be replaced by digital alternatives, of course. However, the shipping, handling, and storage costs of print materials are substantial. One superintendent reported that the total cost of shipping, handling, and storage of such materials approached the cost of the materials themselves.

Most obviously, schools save on storage and shipping costs when they make the conversion to digital content for supplemental materials, when appropriate. While difficult to quantify, teacher time savings is also realized when using technology. These savings are substantial. Teacher efficiency improves because technology allows every question, picture, and chunk of text to be easily incorporated into lessons, regardless of the source. It's worth noting that many teachers say they spend a significant amount of time searching for relevant resources.

Moreover, schools can access millions of free online supplemental resources at no charge. One school district experienced a drop in supplemental materials cost per student from $79 to $19 after switching to digital content.

Student interest should not be overlooked when examining the benefits of providing supplemental materials in digital formats. Simply put, digital materials appeal to today's students and build student engagement, which is key to academic success.

- **National-level savings.** $1.7 billion, based on $31 per student per year.

Digital versus Print Core Curriculum

Digital core curriculum has the potential to save money in reduced printing, transportation, and storage costs. In addition, these materials have the potential to be much more customized and deliver content that is much richer. Textbook costs receive a lot of attention, probably out of proportion to their relative share of the budget. The national textbook budget is estimated to be $4.2 billion, or $76 per student per year.

Because high-quality digital core curriculum materials can be more expensive to produce than textbooks, and because printing and shipping are less than 25% of the cost of a textbook, the immediate savings of a switch from print to digital are limited. However, the switch enables a transformation of the classroom that is, ultimately, the source of significant long-term savings.

The trend to smaller high schools means that there are fewer students per class in honors and AP courses. The cost per student in these classes could be double the cost of a student in a regular class, because one teacher is teaching fewer students. Switching from print to digital formats can help offset this cost. Perhaps more importantly, there are significant financial benefits attributable to AP classes because of reduced state subsidies to colleges, and because students graduate earlier.

Moreover, schools can contract with a virtual school that is responsible for student access to courses, technology devices, infrastructure, and teachers. Student engagement improves because of the personalized learning experience provided by digital content. This leads to more course completion, increased graduation rates, and other benefits. In addition, online course delivery addresses the shortage of qualified teachers as well as the demand for additional course offerings, all of which have financial implications.

- **National-level savings.** $935 million per year, based on savings of $17 per student per year.

Online Professional Learning

Professional learning is critical to the success of any school. Online professional learning has the potential to offer a more customized learning experience, which can meet the specific needs of each teacher in terms of time, place, and content. While some face-to-face professional learning is essential, it is the most expensive form of professional learning, and many would argue it is the least efficient.

In the study *America's Digital Schools 2006* (Greaves & Hayes, 2006), respondents reported spending an average of $100 per student for professional learning in 1-to-1 schools. Urban school districts in another study (Miles, Odden, Fermanich, & Archibald, 2004) reported spending an average of $4,350 per teacher.

Transportation costs are reduced or eliminated when teachers no longer have to travel to on-site trainings. Savings in travel translates to reductions in fees for substitute teachers, consulting services, and other expenses.

Research tells us that reflection, discussion, and coaching are essential for effective adult learning. Negative teacher attitudes toward professional learning, which are widespread, improve when teachers can select courses of personal interest, learn at their own pace, and communicate with colleagues. Online professional learning provides just such an experience. This learning includes courses or workshops that are synchronous (real-time collaboration and communication) and asynchronous (time-lag collaboration and communication), and provides online professional learning communities.

- **National-level savings.** $660 million, based on $12 per student per year.

Power Savings

The electricity costs of a single computer may appear to be trivial, but the cumulative cost of electricity for all computers in a school can be substantial. Desktop computers consume substantially more electricity than do laptops or other handheld computing devices.

The electricity to power one student desktop computer and display costs about $80 per year, or $400 over five years. At the current national average of three students per computer, the approximate cost of desktop computer power is $26 per student per year. Currently 52% of computers in schools are desktops.

The electricity to power one student laptop costs about $11 a year or $55 over five years. For students who switch from a desktop computer to a laptop, the savings is $15 per student. Netbooks cost less because they require less power. iPads and Android-based tablets use significantly less power than a netbook. If students charge their laptops at home, the savings are higher.

- **National-level savings.** $429 million per year, based on $15 per student per year, assuming 52% of students switch from desktop to laptop computer.

Space Savings

The use of space in schools has come under increasing scrutiny over the past few years, with an increased focus on designing schools to support improved learning and simultaneously cut costs. The transition to mobile computing can lead to fewer dedicated computer labs.

A 30-foot-by-30-foot computer lab costs $150,000 or more to construct, including the extra wiring, furniture, and air conditioning, for an amortized annual cost of about $17 per student, not including the computers. Four computers in the back of a classroom require about 125 extra square feet of space, at $100 per square foot. These computers also require Ethernet cable drops and power drops at a cost of several hundred dollars per computer.

Equipped with Wi-Fi–enabled laptops, students can transform a common area or cafeteria into an online learning lab in minutes. There is no need for a computer lab or dedicated space in the back of each classroom. In most cases, a cart of laptops can replace a computer lab. Eliminating a computer lab also means schools also save on air-conditioning costs. (Given the wide variation in schools and climates, calculations are not provided here.) Henrico County Public Schools, for example, reported a reduction of one computer lab per school after moving to a 1-to-1 implementation.

- **National-level savings.** $825 million, based on $15 or more per student per year. Actual savings will vary based on occupancy rates.

Student Data Mapping

Schools collect a substantial amount of data on students and performance. The Race to the Top funding criteria include numerous requirements for statewide longitudinal data systems to capture data from one grade to the next, measure whether students are on track to graduate, indicate whether schools are preparing students to succeed, reward successful teachers, and help struggling teachers improve.

Student data is often collected and entered many times by many people, including teachers, principals, school staff, and district staff, resulting in duplicated and wasted effort. The Project RED team estimates the current cost of acquiring, cleaning, archiving, and accessing student data at $50 per student per year.

Districts that are mapping student data can reduce manual data acquisition and archival work by 30%. This substantial savings comes about when districts more effectively use their current student management information software to reduce the cost of acquiring, archiving, and accessing student information by a mere 20%.

Districts can transfer those savings to other budget areas that are closer to students. Project RED has estimated a savings range of $100,000 to $300,000 per district. The cost avoidance range varies depending on district size and level of implementation. These estimates were obtained from conversations with Holly Area Schools (3,947 students as of September 2008), Waterford School District (11,468 students as of September 2008), and Hillsdale County Intermediate School District (6,840 students as of August 2009) in Michigan. In addition, these districts have created a platform upon which to review student-mapping protocols with software providers, thus accelerating the use of technology in streamlining organizational processes.

- **National-level savings.** $605 million annually, based on an average savings of $11 per student per year.

Summary of Potential Savings

The accompanying table shows the national savings, calculated by multiplying the average savings by 55 million students. The results are sorted by level of savings, from low to high.

Annual National Financial Impact:
The Potential of Technology Transformation in U.S. K–12 Schools

Category	National Impact	Per Student
Student data mapping	$605,000,000	$11
Online professional learning	$660,000,000	$12
Teacher attendance increase	$715,000,000	$13
Space savings	$825,000,000	$15
Power savings*	$429,000,000	$15
Digital core curriculum savings	$935,000,000	$17
Disciplinary action reduction	$1,100,000,000	$20
Post-secondary remedial education	$1,650,000,000	$30
Digital supplemental materials vs. print	$1,705,000,000	$31
Copy machine cost calculations	$2,200,000,000	$40
Online assessment savings	$2,420,000,000	$44
Dual/joint/AP course enrollment	$3,190,000,000	$58
Paperwork reduction	$3,300,000,000	$60
End-of-course failure	$5,885,000,000	$107
Subtotal	**$25,619,000,000**	**$473**
1-to-1 Technology cost savings†	**−$16,225,000,000**	**−$295**
Net Savings	$9,394,000,000	**$178**
Dropout rate reduction‡	$3,095,015,000,000	$56,273
Total	**$3,104,409,000,000**	**$56,451**

* Savings apply only to the 52% of students who are still using desktop computers.

† Net savings between a 1-to-1 technology installation ($593 per student) and a 3-to-1 technology installation ($298 per student).

‡ The financial impact of dropout prevention continues for many years. When potential dropouts graduate from college, the benefit is delayed for several years after their high school graduation and increased tax revenues continue throughout their careers. Another graduating class starts contributing each year, and the per-year impact rises. After 40 years or so, the contributions reach a steady state. The net impact after steady state is $3 trillion per year, not indexed for inflation and other effects. This number is obtained by multiplying the net increases in tax revenues for high school and college graduates by 10% of dropouts who are projected to complete a college degree by an expected working career of 40 years.

Source: Project RED (www.projectred.org)

Conclusion

It is important to keep in mind that there are other categories of savings not included here. One topic that receives frequent mention but is not included in this study is the cost of incarceration. Some states even forecast prison growth requirements based on third grade reading levels.

Project RED's research indicates that we can address two of the biggest challenges facing our society. We can have a better-educated populace. And if we implement programs correctly, in the long term we can generate additional revenue at the state level that far exceeds the total cost of the educational system. To our knowledge, this is the first time that the potential cost-savings impact of properly implemented educational technology has been comprehensively estimated.

CHAPTER 10

NextSchools:
A Vision for the 21st Century

Imagine a new breed of schools where the objective is to double the rate of learning, and the primary characteristic is a relentless focus on personalization and student-centricity. Imagine a new breed of schools where achievement is constant, while, at the same time, if students need more time to master a particular subject, they get it.

This new vision of schools, conceived of by the authors and based on the Project RED findings, is known as NextSchool.

Overview

NextSchool students move at their own pace. NextSchools are designed to facilitate self-directed and self-paced learning, and to minimize the amount of time that progress is not being made. Robust formative assessments are part of the daily routine at a NextSchool, and these assessments provide just-in-time information for students and teachers to support adjustments and remediation.

Online subject-specific experts, as well as mentors and trainers, are available to support the NextSchool's classroom teacher if needed. Productive partnerships with the community, business, and industry fuel a relevant, real-world approach to teaching and learning concepts and skills throughout the curriculum.

Grades K–8

The NextSchool curriculum delves as deeply as possible into each concept and skill using inquiry, and problem- and project-based research scenarios. Average students today read two million words by the end of eighth grade, and high-performing students read four million words. In a NextSchool, every student reads a minimum of four million words, and students enter high school with the foundation for literacy success.

Grades 9–12

The emphasis here is on individualized education plans that are tied to an individualized curriculum, and unique goals and aspirations. Core subjects are pursued in a deep, personalized manner. Students may elect to take courses tailored for future careers, such as health care, information technology, engineering, manufacturing, or journalism. Content is tied to real-life problems, issues, and experiences, and is tailored to students' unique plans.

The Carnegie unit and related seat time are replaced by the demonstration of skill and knowledge related to personalized goals and plans. Most students pursue higher education courses (one course in Grade 9, two in Grade 10, and so on) via dual enrollment, advanced placement, internships, and externships, as well as coursework online and inside and outside the school walls. The strategic partner organizations provide mentors or guides.

Students who are not ready for higher education receive remediation in high school or earlier. Given the deeper learning and higher standards for course completion, remedial courses and their related costs are reduced dramatically. Remediation becomes the exception rather than the norm.

First- and Second-Order Change

NextSchools attempt to realize a second-order change in K–12 education. (See Chapter 1 for an examination of orders of change.) The question is not whether we must change, but how to effect those changes to meet the realities of our world today.

An example of profound technological changes from another era illustrates what we mean by orders of change in building NextSchools. The Pony Express mail service is famed lore of the American West. It operated for a mere 18 months from 1860 to 1861. It did not simply appear and then disappear. Rather, it grew out of a freight delivery operation beginning a decade earlier that delivered supplies to the western frontier. The freight operators had established existing trade routes, and determined mounted riders could shorten transit times over existing routes and provide a fast mail service between St. Joseph, Missouri, and Sacramento, California. Delivery time for a letter was 10 days at $5 per half ounce. And, for those 18 short months, the Pony Express service provided speed and efficiency that were previously unimaginable. Then came two new technologies representing second-order change: the first was fast, dependable mail and package delivery by train, and then came the telegraph, a startling new technology that made communicating messages across great distances easy and almost instantaneous.

We can draw any number of parallels to the Pony Express of 1860 and the ever-changing nature of today's technologies. But instead of focusing on the differences of two different technologies (fast mail delivery by horse-mounted rider versus ultra-fast communication by telegraph wire), let us consider the change within one of the technologies. In this way we can best illustrate the nature of first- and second-order change.

When the Pony Express introduced faster horses, better horse feed, and lighter-weight papers, the incremental improvements in speed constituted a first-order change. Then the telegraph provided a second-order change. Note, however, that even with the advent of the telegraph, a completely different and in many ways superior technology, mail service did not disappear. Rather, each technology found its place and then changed accordingly over time. Mail service continues to this day, of course, though with unheard-of efficiency compared to the late 1800s. Likewise, the telegraph service of the late 1800s is no more, although its spirit remains in the Internet exchanges of today.

With examples of first- and second-order change in mind, let us consider a few illustrations that describe change in our schools today. In so doing, we shall see how change today can lead us to the NextSchools of tomorrow.

Educational Examples

Using a computer program to run flash cards is a first-order change. If the program is adaptive and shows students only the cards they need to see, then some time can be reallocated to improving performance in other areas. This is an improvement, but still a first-order change.

A system that tracks all the students all the time can use advanced analytics to pinpoint the root causes of lack of progress and provide remediation. Identification of the skills not learned and an accelerated teaching and learning cycle lead to a more efficient learning environment and greater cost-effectiveness—a second-order change.

Let's look at another example. If students receive assignments and turn them in via the learning management system (LMS) rather than on paper, the school enjoys savings in copying costs and teacher time—a nice first-order change. If schools move to digital instructional materials, the cost of copying blackline masters is reduced. Schools can also see which materials are actually used, by whom, and when. And they can adjust purchasing requests to minimize costs—this is a first-order change that could set the stage for second-order change.

Best of all, with an LMS, use of instructional materials can be tied to student performance over large sample sizes, insight can be gained into what works for which populations, and the most effective materials can be automatically deployed on a student-by-student basis. Learning what works for specific populations can dramatically reduce the cost of remediation by personalizing instruction. If schools know what works, they reduce purchases of redundant products and services. This is a second-order change.

Conclusion

The NextSchool concept addresses the need to revolutionize the way we look at technology as part of teaching and learning. We believe that technology can help us reengineer our educational system. We believe that technology can and should transform learning, just as it has transformed homes and offices in almost every other segment of our society. We believe that, properly implemented, technology will lead to radical, second-order changes in education! And we hope this book will serve as your roadmap, no matter where you are in your journey.

APPENDIX A

About Project RED

Project RED began with the big idea that the re-engineering of American education could revolutionize our schools. Because the idea that technology enhances learning is not a provable hypothesis, the Project RED team focused on investigating the dramatic gains and cost savings achieved by some schools when they deploy technology. The Project RED team wanted to determine how widespread the improvements were and to what degree the frequent use of technology was a factor.

Research Methodology

Project RED data is derived from a survey of education professionals. Project RED follows standard survey methodology in that questions were asked of a population and relationships between the variables were studied. However, the population studied did not come from a stratified sample of all U.S. public schools, but rather from a self-selected sample of public- and private-school professionals who responded to a variety of outbound messages. To determine the level of representation, the respondents were compared with their counterparts in the public-school universe.

Initial Plan

The initial research design of Project RED was based on the assumption that a study of 1-to-1 schools would yield insights and distinctions among schools that had made the investment in technology necessary to provide continuous access for each student.

Database Development

A database of all U.S. schools, both public and private, was obtained from MDR, a D&B Company that maintains the most robust database of schools in the nation. The initial target audience was school principals and technology coordinators in schools that are implementing robust technology programs. Responses were solicited from principals and technology directors in order to collect data from administrators close to the student. Project RED focused on a data set of schools identified as having more than 100 students and a 1.3-to-1 or lower ratio of students to computers. Although the intent was to identify schools with a 1-to-1 student–computer ratio, a slightly higher than 1-to-1 number (1.3-to-1) was selected to provide for parents opting out of programs and the difficulty of accurately estimating the rapidly changing number of computing devices in any school.

Survey Design

Project RED was designed to identify the use of various educational technologies by frequency, as well as to identify several academic and financial outcomes.

More Information

For a complete description of the Project RED research methodology and data analysis, the Project RED survey instrument, and related materials to assist in further investigations, please contact the Project RED team at info@projectred.org.

This book is based on *The Technology Factor: Nine Keys to Student Achievement and Cost-Effectiveness,* by T. Greaves, J. Hayes, L. Wilson, M. Gielniak, and R. Peterson (2010; ISBN 1-57953-760-X; published and distributed in partnership with MDR; www.schooldata.com).

Project RED Roadmap Checklist

The following actions are designed to facilitate proper technology implementation.

Leadership

❏ Identify district committee members and meeting schedule.

❏ Identify team leadership.

❏ Schedule district leadership planning sessions (with superintendents, curriculum directors, principals, technology directors, business officials, teacher leaders).

❏ Share and discuss the research on 1-to-1 and large-scale implementations.

❏ Draft the shared vision.

❏ Plan the timeline for building the infrastructure.

❏ Bring district leaders together in Dynamic Technology Planning Program (DTPP) training sessions.

❏ Develop and schedule the professional development plan.

❏ Establish the timeline for building-level training (principals, teachers, technical support, and lead teachers).

❏ Draft the administrative support plan for classroom teachers in pilot and ensuing years.

❏ Schedule and implement orientation plans for all stakeholders.

- ❏ Students
- ❏ Teachers
- ❏ Bus drivers
- ❏ Support staff
- ❏ Parents/guardians
- ❏ Community
- ❏ Plan the outbound communications program to community and parents and guardians.
- ❏ Secure signed acceptable use policies.
- ❏ Identify the assessment plan and timeline.
  - ❏ Create program goals.
  - ❏ Collect baseline data.
  - ❏ Develop assessment protocol and tools.
- ❏ Schedule the implementation timeline.
  - ❏ Wireless network testing
  - ❏ Bandwidth capacity testing in pilot class
  - ❏ Ongoing professional development
  - ❏ Troubleshooting protocol
  - ❏ Technology support protocol
    - ❏ Teachers
    - ❏ Students
    - ❏ Other personnel
    - ❏ Online
    - ❏ Help desk
- ❏ Plan the distribution of devices to students.
- ❏ Schedule site visits.

Technology Infrastructure (Initial Pilot Requirements)

❒ At least one classroom

❒ At least two teachers trained

❒ A laptop for each teacher

❒ A mobile computing device for each student in the classroom

❒ Infrastructure to support pilot

    ❒ Bandwidth

    ❒ Access points

    ❒ Server space

    ❒ Electrical capacity in classroom

❒ On-site technical support

❒ Relationship with vendor

    ❒ Terms of contract

    ❒ Support services

    ❒ Swap out and repair policies

❒ One extra device for every 10 laptops for loaners

❒ A charging cart for each classroom

❒ Two battery packs for each laptop

❒ Accidental damage and theft insurance for all computing devices

Other Beneficial Classroom Technology

❒ LCD projector

❒ Interactive whiteboard

District Infrastructure

❒ An implementation timeline

❒ Enough access points to ensure wireless connectivity for all students in the 1-to-1 learning space

❒ Awareness of how the program might affect other technology users

❒ An appropriate firewall, virus protection, and content filter

❒ Dedicated server space able to handle the capacity of the program (a folder for every student and teacher)

❒ Wireless network testing

❒ Bandwidth capacity testing

❒ Appropriate use policies for the network, the Internet, and mobile computing devices

❒ Appropriate device preparation

   ❒ An accurate drive/disk image

   ❒ Adjustment of all settings

   ❒ A device identification method

   ❒ Loading and testing of all software

❒ A plan for the distribution of devices to students

❒ Enough technology personnel to support the 1-to-1 program

❒ An established relationship with the device vendor and teacher access to the vendor's help desk and other support

❒ A quick-response support plan for repairs and other technical questions that can be easily communicated to teachers

❒ Appropriate damage and theft insurance

National Educational Technology Standards

NETS for Students (NETS•S)

All K–12 students should be prepared to meet the following standards and performance indicators:

1. Creativity and Innovation

Students demonstrate creative thinking, construct knowledge, and develop innovative products and processes using technology. Students:

    a. apply existing knowledge to generate new ideas, products, or processes

    b. create original works as a means of personal or group expression

    c. use models and simulations to explore complex systems and issues

    d. identify trends and forecast possibilities

2. Communication and Collaboration

Students use digital media and environments to communicate and work collaboratively, including at a distance, to support individual learning and contribute to the learning of others. Students:

    a. interact, collaborate, and publish with peers, experts, or others employing a variety of digital environments and media

    b. communicate information and ideas effectively to multiple audiences using a variety of media and formats

    c. develop cultural understanding and global awareness by engaging with learners of other cultures

    d. contribute to project teams to produce original works or solve problems

3. Research and Information Fluency

Students apply digital tools to gather, evaluate, and use information. Students:

    a. plan strategies to guide inquiry

    b. locate, organize, analyze, evaluate, synthesize, and ethically use information from a variety of sources and media

    c. evaluate and select information sources and digital tools based on the appropriateness to specific tasks

    d. process data and report results

4. Critical Thinking, Problem Solving, and Decision Making

Students use critical thinking skills to plan and conduct research, manage projects, solve problems, and make informed decisions using appropriate digital tools and resources. Students:

    a. identify and define authentic problems and significant questions for investigation

    b. plan and manage activities to develop a solution or complete a project

    c. collect and analyze data to identify solutions and/or make informed decisions

    d. use multiple processes and diverse perspectives to explore alternative solutions

5. Digital Citizenship

Students understand human, cultural, and societal issues related to technology and practice legal and ethical behavior. Students:

    a. advocate and practice safe, legal, and responsible use of information and technology

    b. exhibit a positive attitude toward using technology that supports collaboration, learning, and productivity

   c. demonstrate personal responsibility for lifelong learning

   d. exhibit leadership for digital citizenship

6. Technology Operations and Concepts

Students demonstrate a sound understanding of technology concepts, systems, and operations. Students:

   a. understand and use technology systems

   b. select and use applications effectively and productively

   c. troubleshoot systems and applications

   d. transfer current knowledge to learning of new technologies

© 2007 International Society for Technology in Education (ISTE), www.iste.org. All rights reserved.

NETS for Teachers (NETS•T)

All classroom teachers should be prepared to meet the following standards and performance indicators.

1. Facilitate and Inspire Student Learning and Creativity

Teachers use their knowledge of subject matter, teaching and learning, and technology to facilitate experiences that advance student learning, creativity, and innovation in both face-to-face and virtual environments. Teachers:

   a. promote, support, and model creative and innovative thinking and inventiveness

   b. engage students in exploring real-world issues and solving authentic problems using digital tools and resources

   c. promote student reflection using collaborative tools to reveal and clarify students' conceptual understanding and thinking, planning, and creative processes

   d. model collaborative knowledge construction by engaging in learning with students, colleagues, and others in face-to-face and virtual environments

2. Design and Develop Digital-Age Learning Experiences and Assessments

Teachers design, develop, and evaluate authentic learning experiences and assessments incorporating contemporary tools and resources to maximize content learning in context and to develop the knowledge, skills, and attitudes identified in the NETS•S. Teachers:

a. design or adapt relevant learning experiences that incorporate digital tools and resources to promote student learning and creativity

b. develop technology-enriched learning environments that enable all students to pursue their individual curiosities and become active participants in setting their own educational goals, managing their own learning, and assessing their own progress

c. customize and personalize learning activities to address students' diverse learning styles, working strategies, and abilities using digital tools and resources

d. provide students with multiple and varied formative and summative assessments aligned with content and technology standards and use resulting data to inform learning and teaching

3. Model Digital-Age Work and Learning

Teachers exhibit knowledge, skills, and work processes representative of an innovative professional in a global and digital society. Teachers:

a. demonstrate fluency in technology systems and the transfer of current knowledge to new technologies and situations

b. collaborate with students, peers, parents, and community members using digital tools and resources to support student success and innovation

c. communicate relevant information and ideas effectively to students, parents, and peers using a variety of digital-age media and formats

d. model and facilitate effective use of current and emerging digital tools to locate, analyze, evaluate, and use information resources to support research and learning

4. Promote and Model Digital Citizenship and Responsibility

Teachers understand local and global societal issues and responsibilities in an evolving digital culture and exhibit legal and ethical behavior in their professional practices. Teachers:

    a. advocate, model, and teach safe, legal, and ethical use of digital information and technology, including respect for copyright, intellectual property, and the appropriate documentation of sources

    b. address the diverse needs of all learners by using learner-centered strategies and providing equitable access to appropriate digital tools and resources

    c. promote and model digital etiquette and responsible social interactions related to the use of technology and information

    d. develop and model cultural understanding and global awareness by engaging with colleagues and students of other cultures using digital-age communication and collaboration tools

5. Engage in Professional Growth and Leadership

Teachers continuously improve their professional practice, model lifelong learning, and exhibit leadership in their school and professional community by promoting and demonstrating the effective use of digital tools and resources. Teachers:

    a. participate in local and global learning communities to explore creative applications of technology to improve student learning

    b. exhibit leadership by demonstrating a vision of technology infusion, participating in shared decision making and community building, and developing the leadership and technology skills of others

    c. evaluate and reflect on current research and professional practice on a regular basis to make effective use of existing and emerging digital tools and resources in support of student learning

    d. contribute to the effectiveness, vitality, and self-renewal of the teaching profession and of their school and community

© 2008 International Society for Technology in Education (ISTE), www.iste.org. All rights reserved.

NETS for Administrators (NETS•A)

All school administrators should be prepared to meet the following standards and performance indicators.

1. Visionary Leadership

Educational Administrators inspire and lead development and implementation of a shared vision for comprehensive integration of technology to promote excellence and support transformation throughout the organization. Educational Administrators:

   a. inspire and facilitate among all stakeholders a shared vision of purposeful change that maximizes use of digital-age resources to meet and exceed learning goals, support effective instructional practice, and maximize performance of district and school leaders

   b. engage in an ongoing process to develop, implement, and communicate technology-infused strategic plans aligned with a shared vision

   c. advocate on local, state, and national levels for policies, programs, and funding to support implementation of a technology-infused vision and strategic plan

2. Digital-Age Learning Culture

Educational Administrators create, promote, and sustain a dynamic, digital-age learning culture that provides a rigorous, relevant, and engaging education for all students. Educational Administrators:

   a. ensure instructional innovation focused on continuous improvement of digital-age learning

   b. model and promote the frequent and effective use of technology for learning

   c. provide learner-centered environments equipped with technology and learning resources to meet the individual, diverse needs of all learners

   d. ensure effective practice in the study of technology and its infusion across the curriculum

   e. promote and participate in local, national, and global learning communities that stimulate innovation, creativity, and digital-age collaboration

3. Excellence in Professional Practice

Educational Administrators promote an environment of professional learning and innovation that empowers educators to enhance student learning through the infusion of contemporary technologies and digital resources. Educational Administrators:

a. allocate time, resources, and access to ensure ongoing professional growth in technology fluency and integration

b. facilitate and participate in learning communities that stimulate, nurture, and support administrators, faculty, and staff in the study and use of technology

c. promote and model effective communication and collaboration among stakeholders using digital-age tools

d. stay abreast of educational research and emerging trends regarding effective use of technology and encourage evaluation of new technologies for their potential to improve student learning

4. Systemic Improvement

Educational Administrators provide digital-age leadership and management to continuously improve the organization through the effective use of information and technology resources. Educational Administrators:

a. lead purposeful change to maximize the achievement of learning goals through the appropriate use of technology and media-rich resources

b. collaborate to establish metrics, collect and analyze data, interpret results, and share findings to improve staff performance and student learning

c. recruit and retain highly competent personnel who use technology creatively and proficiently to advance academic and operational goals

d. establish and leverage strategic partnerships to support systemic improvement

e. establish and maintain a robust infrastructure for technology including integrated, interoperable technology systems to support management, operations, teaching, and learning

5. Digital Citizenship

Educational Administrators model and facilitate understanding of social, ethical, and legal issues and responsibilities related to an evolving digital culture. Educational Administrators:

a. ensure equitable access to appropriate digital tools and resources to meet the needs of all learners

b. promote, model, and establish policies for safe, legal, and ethical use of digital information and technology

c. promote and model responsible social interactions related to the use of technology and information

d. model and facilitate the development of a shared cultural understanding and involvement in global issues through the use of contemporary communication and collaboration tools

© 2009 International Society for Technology in Education (ISTE), www.iste.org. All rights reserved.

NETS for Coaches (NETS•C)

All technology coaches should be prepared to meet the following standards and performance indicators.

1. Visionary Leadership

Technology Coaches inspire and participate in the development and implementation of a shared vision for the comprehensive integration of technology to promote excellence and support transformational change throughout the instructional environment. Technology Coaches:

a. contribute to the development, communication, and implementation of a shared vision for the comprehensive use of technology to support a digital-age education for all students

b. contribute to the planning, development, communication, implementation, and evaluation of technology-infused strategic plans at the district and school levels

c. advocate for policies, procedures, programs, and funding strategies to support implementation of the shared vision represented in the school and district technology plans and guidelines

    d. implement strategies for initiating and sustaining technology innovations and manage the change process in schools and classrooms

2. Teaching, Learning, and Assessments

Technology Coaches assist teachers in using technology effectively for assessing student learning, differentiating instruction, and providing rigorous, relevant, and engaging learning experiences for all students. Technology Coaches:

    a. Coach teachers in and model design and implementation of technology-enhanced learning experiences addressing content standards and student technology standards

    b. Coach teachers in and model design and implementation of technology-enhanced learning experiences using a variety of research-based, learner-centered instructional strategies and assessment tools to address the diverse needs and interests of all students

    c. Coach teachers in and model engagement of students in local and global interdisciplinary units in which technology helps students assume professional roles, research real-world problems, collaborate with others, and produce products that are meaningful and useful to a wide audience

    d. Coach teachers in and model design and implementation of technology-enhanced learning experiences emphasizing creativity, higher-order thinking skills and processes, and mental habits of mind (e.g., critical thinking, metacognition, and self-regulation)

    e. Coach teachers in and model design and implementation of technology-enhanced learning experiences using differentiation, including adjusting content, process, product, and learning environment based upon student readiness levels, learning styles, interests, and personal goals

    f. Coach teachers in and model incorporation of research-based best practices in instructional design when planning technology-enhanced learning experiences

    g. Coach teachers in and model effective use of technology tools and resources to continuously assess student learning and technology literacy by applying a rich variety of formative and summative assessments aligned with content and student technology standards

    h. Coach teachers in and model effective use of technology tools and resources to systematically collect and analyze student achievement data, interpret results, and communicate findings to improve instructional practice and maximize student learning

3. Digital-Age Learning Environments

Technology coaches create and support effective digital-age learning environments to maximize the learning of all students. Technology Coaches:

a. Model effective classroom management and collaborative learning strategies to maximize teacher and student use of digital tools and resources and access to technology-rich learning environments

b. Maintain and manage a variety of digital tools and resources for teacher and student use in technology-rich learning environments

c. Coach teachers in and model use of online and blended learning, digital content, and collaborative learning networks to support and extend student learning as well as expand opportunities and choices for online professional development for teachers and administrators

d. Select, evaluate, and facilitate the use of adaptive and assistive technologies to support student learning

e. Troubleshoot basic software, hardware, and connectivity problems common in digital learning environments

f. Collaborate with teachers and administrators to select and evaluate digital tools and resources that enhance teaching and learning and are compatible with the school technology infrastructure

g. Use digital communication and collaboration tools to communicate locally and globally with students, parents, peers, and the larger community

4. Professional Development and Program Evaluation

Technology coaches conduct needs assessments, develop technology-related professional learning programs, and evaluate the impact on instructional practice and student learning. Technology Coaches:

a. Conduct needs assessments to inform the content and delivery of technology-related professional learning programs that result in a positive impact on student learning

b. Design, develop, and implement technology-rich professional learning programs that model principles of adult learning and promote digital-age best practices in teaching, learning, and assessment

    c. Evaluate results of professional learning programs to determine their effectiveness on deepening teacher content knowledge, improving teacher pedagogical skills, and/or increasing student learning

5. Digital Citizenship

Technology coaches model and promote digital citizenship. Technology Coaches:

    a. Model and promote strategies for achieving equitable access to digital tools and resources and technology-related best practices for all students and teachers

    b. Model and facilitate safe, healthy, legal, and ethical uses of digital information and technologies

    c. Model and promote diversity, cultural understanding, and global awareness by using digital-age communication and collaboration tools to interact locally and globally with students, peers, parents, and the larger community

6. Content Knowledge and Professional Growth

Technology coaches demonstrate professional knowledge, skills, and dispositions in content, pedagogical, and technological areas, as well as adult learning and leadership, and are continuously deepening their knowledge and expertise. Technology Coaches:

    a. Engage in continual learning to deepen content and pedagogical knowledge in technology integration and current and emerging technologies necessary to effectively implement the NETS•S and NETS•T

    b. Engage in continuous learning to deepen professional knowledge, skills, and dispositions in organizational change and leadership, project management, and adult learning to improve professional practice

    c. Regularly evaluate and reflect on their professional practice and dispositions to improve and strengthen their ability to effectively model and facilitate technology-enhanced learning experiences

References

Belfield, C. & Levin, H. M. (2007). *The price we pay: Economic and social consequences of inadequate education.* Washington, DC: Brookings Institution.

Cuban, L. (1988). *The managerial imperative and the practice of leadership in schools.* Albany, NY: State Universtiy of New York.

Greaves Group, Hayes Connection, & One-to-One Institute (2010). *The technology factor: Nine keys to student achievement and cost-effectiveness.* Shelton, CT: MDR.

Greaves, T. & Hayes, J. (2006). *America's digital schools 2006.* Shelton, CT: MDR.

Greaves, T. & Hayes, J. (2008). *America's digital schools 2008.* Shelton, CT: MDR.

Marzano, R. J., Waters, T., & McNulty, B. A., (2005). *School leadership that works: From research to results.* Aurora, CO: McREL.

Miles, K. H., Odden, A., Fermanich, M., & Archibald, S. (2004). Inside the black box of school district spending on professional development: Lessons from five urban districts. *Journal of Education Finance, 30*(1), 1–25.

Project RED. (n.d.). [Website]. www.projectred.org